# THE OH, CANADIANS! OMNIBUS!

## Hysterically Historical Rhymes

GORDON SNELL

*With caricatures by*
AISLIN

McArthur & Company
Toronto

FIRST PRINTING

National Library of Canadian Cataloguing in Publication Data


Snell, Gordon
The Oh, Canadians! omnibus

ISBN 1–55278–254–9

1. Celebrities – Canada – Poetry. 2. Humorous poetry, English.
3. Canadian wit and humor, Pictorial. I. Aislin. II. Title.


PR6069.N440533 2001      821'.914      C2001–901667–0

Cover Illustration by *AISLIN*
Layout, Design and Electronic Imaging by *MARY HUGHSON*
Printed and Bound in Canada by
*TRANSCONTINENTAL PRINTING, TORONTO*

## McArthur & Company

Toronto

322 KING STREET WEST, SUITE 402, TORONTO,
ONTARIO, CANADA, M5V 1J2

The publisher would like to acknowledge the financial support of the
Government of Canada through the Book Publishing Industry Development
Program (BPIDP) and the Canada Council for our publishing activities.
The publisher further wishes to acknowledge the financial support of the
Ontario Arts Council for our publishing program.

10 9 8 7 6 5 4 3 2 1

*These rhymes I give in dedication*
*To Maeve, my love and inspiration*

*GS*


*For Mary,*
*And that hammock in Puerto.*

*A*

# THE OH, CANADIANS! OMNIBUS
## Hysterically Historical Rhymes

# Contents

# THE LOON

*The Loon, featured on the Canadian dollar coin, is one
of the world's oldest birds. It nests on lakes and rivers,
and is known for its weird and distinctive calls.*

Sing a song of sixpence
And never mind the tune.
We've got a dollar coin here
To celebrate the Loon.

Loons deserve your praises
Loons deserve your cheers
Loons have been around now
At least ten thousand years!

We can sound like wolves do
Howling in the night.
Even when we're laughing
It gives them all a fright.

Our portrait's on the coinage
Which ought to make us glad
But they're calling it the Loonie
Which really makes us mad!

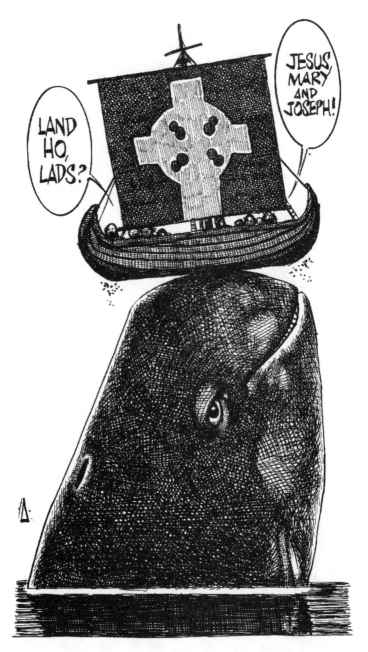

# SAINT BRENDAN
## (484 – 578)

*Brendan was an Irish monk whose voyages to exotic lands were described in a Latin narrative translated and circulated widely in Europe. Many people believe his journeys took him as far as the American continent.*

The Europeans who claim to be
The first, America to see —
Columbus, Cabot, Viking Leif —
May find their claims have come to grief.
There's one who says that First they ain't,
And he is Brendan, Sailor Saint.

That he was real, you can't debunk:
He was a holy Irish monk
Born fifteen centuries ago.
He founded monasteries, we know —
And from a Latin text we learn he
Made the most amazing journey.

Saint Brendan's voyage was designed
The Land of Promise for to find.
He'd dreamed of it, and had, they say,
Bizarre adventures on the way.

They saw upon one island's coasts
Birds that were really hordes of ghosts.

Towards a crystal tower they came,
Then to a mountain, belching flame,
An isle of giants, a curdled sea,
An isle with fruit on every tree;
A rock where Judas had his station,
Let off, on Sundays, from Damnation.

And then they found the boat was beached:
Another isle they must have reached.
But soon the land began to rise:
It was a whale, of giant size.

The boat upon its back was stranded.
The Saint just said: "Well, since we've landed,
This chance we monks must not let pass:
We'll gather round, and say a Mass!"
And when the Mass was done, the whale
Sank down, and Brendan's ship set sail.

The tale's interpretation varies:
Some say he went to the Canaries,
To Iceland, and the Faroes too;
But others take a bolder view:
They say that Brendan's holy band
Went on as far as Newfoundland.

Tim Severin thought so, set afloat
A replica of Brendan's boat,
And though the weather was atrocious
The coast he reached was Nova Scotia's!

The day may come when we shall find
Some object Brendan left behind:
A Celtic cross, some rosary beads —
That sort of find is all it needs
To make all other claimants yield
And prove Saint Brendan led the field!

# LEIF ERICCSON
## (died 1020)

*According to the Viking sagas, Leif Ericcson crossed the Atlantic,*
*and the lands he visited are probably Baffin Island and Labrador,*
*and finally Vinland, which could be Newfoundland.*

The average marauding Viking
Seized any land that took his liking.
No place was safe in early days
From Scandinavian forays.

Eric the Red first got a taste
To settle Greenland's icy waste,
And soon Leif Ericcson, his son,
His own great journeys had begun.

Over a thousand years ago
He was the first, the sagas show,
Who came from European lands
To step upon Canadian strands.
For those who watched those tall prows rise on
The empty, faraway horizon,
They must have made a curious sight
With spears and helmets gleaming bright.

To Baffin Island, where Leif came,
"The Land of Stones" he gave the name.

"The Wooded Land" he called the shore
Of what we know as Labrador.

In "Vinland" next that crew arrived,
And there the winter they survived.
They found there everything they wished:
Good pastures, salmon to be fished,
And even berries, grapes and vines —
That's why Leif called it "Land of Wines."

Though Vinland's written into history,
Its whereabouts is still a mystery.
Some choose Cape Cod, but others say
It's further north, near Hudson Bay;
And others claim they understand
It's on the coast of Newfoundland.

It must have been, if that is so,
Much warmer, centuries ago.
If only it had stayed that way,
We might be all enjoying today
The Newfoundlanders' Chardonnay.

But as it is, they've found their niche
With something stronger: pass the SCREECH!

# JOHN CABOT
## (1425 – c.1500)

*Originally from Italy, John Cabot went to England to get backing*
*from King Henry VII and the merchants of Bristol to search*
*for a sea route to Asia. He was the first of the explorers of that*
*period to land on the North American continent.*

For navigators, like John Cabot,
Ocean trips became a habit.
From youth, he heard the waters call —
He was Venetian, after all.

But Bristol merchants, and the King,
Financed John Cabot's journeying.
In 1497, he
Aboard the Matthew went to sea.
He reached the coast, we understand,
Most probably in Newfoundland.
In fact, the date he landed on
Was at the feast day of St John.

He raised a flag, in England's name,
Set several snares to capture game,
And said: "Lest anyone forgets,
I'll leave this needle too, for nets —
Then passers-by will be advised
This place is truly colonised."

No doubt the people living there
Were not aware, or didn't care
That he had come to their locality
And claimed to change their nationality!

More vital was the news he bore
Of oceans full of fish galore:
For Cabot on the way had found
The future Grand Banks fishing ground.

Though people praise Columbus more
For his trip, just five years before,
That sailor, after many dramas,
Had only got to the Bahamas;
While Cabot, with the same intent,
At least had reached the Continent.

Yet both explorers never ceased
To think that they had reached the East.
They didn't know, like us today,
America was in the way!

# JACQUES CARTIER
## (1491 – 1557)

*Jacques Cartier was the first European to explore the Gulf of St. Lawrence and the St. Lawrence River. His encounters with the Iroquois ranged from friendship to hostility, and the treasure he finally brought home was not what he expected.*

"Sail west!" Jacques Cartier was told,
"And find me countries rich in gold."
The King of France had spoken, so
Jacques thought he'd really better go.
Besides, it was a mission which
With any luck, would make him rich.

He crossed the ocean, but he found
That Labrador was barren ground.
He treated it with some abhorrence —
But then he came to the St. Lawrence.
He crossed the Gulf, and made his way
Along the coast to Gaspé Bay.

And there he managed to annoy
The friendly local Iroquois
By putting up a giant cross
To show them all just who was Boss.

Chief Donnacona wasn't pleased —
But strained relations soon were eased.

It was Jacques' Gallic charm, we think —
Or was there something in the drink?
At any rate, Jacques took the chance
To ask the Chief's two sons to France.

The next year, when he brought them back,
They helped to put him on the track:
They showed him the St. Lawrence River.
"What riches I can now deliver!"
Exclaimed Jacques Cartier, as they told
Of distant kingdoms, full of gold.

He also thought the river went
Right through into the Orient.
And so, continuing his saga,
He sailed right on, to Hochelaga.

There, he was joyfully received.
He'd cure the sick, they all believed.
He read the Gospel of St John,
And though their pains and aches weren't gone,
They kindly didn't swear and curse:
At least, he hadn't made them worse.

A nearby mountain he did name,
And Mont-Royal it then became —
Now Montreal, the very same.
Then winter came, and scurvy too.
No Gospel cured that, Cartier knew.
The Iroquois' white-cedar brew

Was what saved most of Cartier's crew.

No thanks they got, but only grief:
In spring Jacques came and seized their Chief.
He took ten other prisoners too.
"I'll bring them back as good as new!"
That's what he promised, but we know
His vows all melted, with the snow.

To Canada the navigator
Did not return till six years later.
This time, he built a settlement:
To colonize was his intent.
But he was even more delighted
When gold and diamonds were sighted.

He thought that they'd be valued highly
And he would live the life of Riley.
But back in France, he found the ore
Was iron pyrites, nothing more,
And learned from valuers' reports
His diamonds were only quartz.

At least, the jewellers today
Have saved the name of CARTIER!

# SAMUEL DE CHAMPLAIN
## (1570-1635)

*Samuel de Champlain was an enthusiastic explorer
and map-maker who founded France's first colony in the
New World at Quebec in 1608.*

Champlain was eager to advance
His country's glory, in New France.
The best maps of the region then,
Came from his cartographic pen.
From Port-Royal, his earliest post,
He mapped the whole New England coast.

Explorers' trips, he realized,
Were best if locally advised.
So he made friendships, for insurance,
With the Algonquins and the Hurons.
When with these tribes his friendship grew
He travelled with them by canoe
And that was how he came to know
Lakes Huron and Ontario.
Then at another lake, said he:
"Let's call it Champlain, after me !"

Samuel was brave - among his stunts,
He shot the rapids, more than once.

Champlain was able to persuade
The French King that enormous trade
Would flow, if colonies were made.
He even thought it would be cute
When someone found the China route
To have on the Atlantic coast
A lucrative French Customs post.

After much thought, he chose the lands
Just in the place Quebec now stands.
His plans at first went topsy-turvy
When many settlers died of scurvy,
But Champlain never had a doubt:
He grew wheat, made a pool for trout,
And had a grand town plan laid out.

To make the winters seem less drear
He formed the Order of Good Cheer.
They'd hunt game for the festive table
And drink as much as they were able.

In transatlantic sailing ships
Champlain made over twenty trips,
And after one, he would decide:
"I'm forty - time I took a bride!"
The records, though, have never told
Just why he chose one, twelve years old.

Nor why, despite a happy life
In due course, with his grown-up wife,

He chose at last his will to vary
And leave all to the Virgin Mary.

He was  exceedingly devout
And brought religious orders out
Among the tribes to make excursions
Attempting to promote conversions.

His colony survived a check -
The English capture of Quebec.
But then another deal was done:
Champlain was back, as Number One.
If thwarted, he cried: "Sacre Bleu! -
I'm here to act for Richelieu!"

He died, to solemn lamentation,
Where his first humble habitation
Had founded the Canadian nation.

# HENRY HUDSON
## (died 1611)

*Henry Hudson, who gave his name to so many places, made four voyages searching for a northern route to the Pacific and China, and was finally cast adrift in an open boat by his rebellious crew.*

Henry Hudson several times
Tried to sail to Eastern climes
Searching for the Isles of Spice,
But was always foiled by ice.

People thought the route northeast
Would lead to China at the least,
But up among the Arctic seas
Hudson found not one Chinese.

On the third trip, Hudson's men,
Ice-bound, grumbled: "Not again!"
A mutiny was in the air,
But Hudson fixed them with a glare:
"Well, if you feel like that," he said,
"We'll turn and sail northwest, instead!"
It made the sailors much less frantic,
Sailing over the Atlantic.

Up the Hudson River then
To Albany he took his men,

Thus showing that this waterway
Could be a trading route one day.
"Whatever this new land has got,"
Said Hudson, "China it is not!"

And so next year, in 1610,
Henry Hudson sailed again.
The spicy Orient was beckoning —
From the west, by Hudson's reckoning.

He believed that Davis Strait
Would be the Northwest Passage gate,
And lead him to an Arctic Sea
Which from drifting ice was free.
But the tide, so fierce and great,
Swept him to another Strait:
The one named Hudson, after him —
Though then, his fate was looking grim.

The crew began to rage and curse,
But turning round would just be worse.
Through icy seas they made their way
Four hundred miles, at ten per day,
Emerging into Hudson Bay.
Henry Hudson felt terrific:
He thought he'd entered the Pacific!

So south they sailed, and found James Bay,
Thinking that China lay that way.
Hudson searched for many days

But found the coast was like a maze.
And then there came the winter snows,
And all the land and waters froze.

Although they built a house on shore,
The winter chilled them to the core.
Now and then they caught some game,
But the dreaded scurvy came
And Henry Hudson got the blame.

When the ice broke up, they sailed:
Though the China trip had failed,
Hudson at the least could say
He'd discovered Hudson Bay.

But he never got the chance —
The others looked at him askance,
And what really roused their passions
Was finding Hudson's hidden rations.

After that, he got short shrift:
Rebels cast a boat adrift
With Hudson and eight men on board.
The rest cried: "That is your reward!"

A mystery surrounds the ends
Of Henry Hudson and his friends,
Left in the icy seas to float
In a leaky open boat.
Bligh kept such a group together,

But he had rather warmer weather!

Hudson, though, could not survive —
And yet his name remains alive:
The Bay, the Company, the Strait,
And towns and rivers, make him great.
But dying of cold and of starvation,
Great fame is not much consolation.

# PETER EASTON
## (early 17th century)

*Peter Easton's swashbuckling energy and cheery personality made
him one of the most colourful pirate leaders of his time. Choosing
Newfoundland as his base, he plundered so many vessels that he
made a fortune, escaping all pursuit with such success that he was
called with some admiration "The Pirate Admiral".*

*(These verses match the tune of the old sea-shanty,
"Bobby Shafto went to sea")*

Peter Easton went to sea
Sword and pistol on his knee
"I'm a Pirate King, that's me!"
    Boasted Peter Easton.

He had ten ships fine and grand
Piracy was what he planned
When he came to Newfoundland
    "Admiral" Peter Easton.

There at Harbour Grace he stayed
Up and down the coast he'd raid
"There's a fortune to be made!"
    Gloated Peter Easton.

Fishermen to join him came
Drawn to him by loot and fame

Many of them took his name,
　　Praising Peter Easton.

Scores of vessels he did seize,
English, French and Portuguese,
Plundering them all with ease,
　　How they hated Easton!

To Cuper's Cove he made a trip
Took a merchant in his grip
Kept him weeks on board his ship
　　Crafty Peter Easton.

Then he said: "I'll set you free
If you'll tell the powers-that-be:
'Send a pardon here to me,
　　Here to Peter Easton.' "

Newfoundland admired him most –
Now he planned to be the toast
Of the Riviera Coast,
　　Showy Peter Easton.

There he lived in wealth and fame
But Newfoundland to which he came
Still has many an Easton name -
　　Praising Peter Easton.

# ROBERT CAVELIER DE LA SALLE
## (1643-1687)

*La Salle crossed the Atlantic to New France with an ambition to explore and to grow rich. He achieved these aims, but not entirely successfully, since he both found - and lost - the Mississippi.*

La Salle, a would-be Jesuit,
After nine years was asked to quit.
Sulking, he said: "I'll take a chance
And try my fortune in New France."

A man devoid of inhibition,
He joined up with an expedition,
Telling the leaders: "I'm your boy,
For I  speak fluent Iroquois."

His claim was shown to be absurd -
He couldn't understand a word.
But he declared: "I'll soon be back!"
And Governor General Frontenac
To whom he showed extreme servility
Promoted him to the nobility.

Back home in France, at Court he schemed
To clinch the deal of which he dreamed,
And soon two clerics with ambition
Helped get La Salle an expedition.

Then joyfully he shouted: "Yipee!
I'll sail right down the Mississippi!"

And so La Salle went sailing south
Right down the river to its mouth.
He then dressed up, so we are told,
In robes of scarlet and of gold
And stated: "I did everything
For Louis, France's glorious King.
He's now the Lord of this Nirvana -
Let's call the place LOUISIANA!"

The fur trade made his fortune grow;
His fort on Lake Ontario
And other ventures made La Salle
A V.I.P. in *Montréal.*

Then being a devious sort of chap
He showed the King a bogus map
Charting the Mississippi's flow
Far west of where it ought to go.
He told the King: "With this, it's true,
We'll conquer Mexico for you!"

He meant to land as he intended,
Just where the Mississippi ended;
But though he'd sailed it all before
He couldn't find it any more.
He told his party: "I'm afraid
The Mississippi's been mislaid!"

So up and down the coast they sailed
To seek the Delta, but they failed.
Sensing his men were in a tizz
La Salle said smoothly: "Here it is!"

They said: "This guy begins to vex us -
This, clearly, is the coast of Texas.
And we're so weary and sick of trying,
And while you're living, you'll go on lying -
Your Old Man River may disappear
But your own end is getting near.
Your fortunes now have reached rock bottom."
With that, they stood him up and shot him.

Considering La Salle's behaviour,
His claims to be their guide and saviour,
His grasping greed and his cupidity,
His treachery and sheer stupidity,
We all might wonder more and more
Just why he wasn't killed before!

# JAMES WOLFE
## (1727 – 1759)

*James Wolfe reached the height of his military career in 1759 when
he was made commander of the British land forces in the expedition
against the French in Quebec.. Though the attack succeeded, both
he and the French general, Montcalm, died in the battle.*

Wolfe started young — at just fourteen,
He first joined up as a Marine.
Perhaps it was coincidence
That out, of all the regiments,
The one that took him in was led
By James's father, at its head.

Marines for Infantry James swapped,
And then his progress never stopped.
He fought in Scotland, Belgium, France,
And then he got his biggest chance.

At Louisbourg he helped attack
The French ships, which were firing back;
He captured some, put some to flame,
And in that battle made his name.
Commander was his next position,
To take Quebec his army's mission.

The French defence force was Montcalm's:
Wolfe faced him without any qualms.

For James, in planning every fight,
Believed that he was always right —
A fact which often, it appears,
Caused quarrels with his Brigadiers.

Wolfe changed his plans throughout that summer:
Some were inspired, some rather dumber.
His main intention, though, was sound:
To tempt Montcalm to open ground.
But that sly General rightly thought:
"My fortress is a safer spot."

At last, and after several tries,
The British troops achieved surprise.
Boats full of soldiers, undetected,
Made landings where they weren't expected.
Beneath the cliffs, at dead of night,
They came ashore, and scaled the height.

Montcalm was now in quite a jam
There on the Plains of Abraham.
His enemy was growing stronger —
He knew that he could wait no longer.

So out he went; some progress made,
The French then met a fusillade.
The furious bombardment stunned them:
British forces had outgunned them.

Montcalm directed a retreat,
But never lived to see defeat:
A fatal bullet struck him down.
Wolfe never saw the captured town —
Although he reached the very portal,
The wounds that he received were mortal.
Quebec surrendered, but the war
Continued for a few years more.

The conquerors in this aggression
Were doubtful of their new possession.
So vast, so troublesome, so cold —
Was this a land they'd want to hold?
And some officials seemed to feel
To give it back had more appeal:
The French might think it quite a scoop
To swap the place for Guadeloupe...

And Canada, with that entente,
Would have une histoire différente!

# JAMES McGILL
## (1744 – 1813)

*James McGill came from Scotland to join the fur trade in Canada.*
*He became a leading merchant and a civic figure in Montreal,*
*where he founded the university that bears his name.*

Canada lured lots and lots
Of young and enterprising Scots,
And one from Glasgow felt the call
To come and live in Montreal.
His name is celebrated still:
He was the famous James McGill.

His University, begun
Way back in 1821,
Has nurtured many brilliant students
Of literature, and jurisprudence
For science, too, its classes cater —
In fact, no accolade is greater
Than saying: "McGill's my Alma Mater!"

Glasgow was where James went to college:
He had an early thirst for knowledge
And entered there, so we are told,
When he was only twelve years old.

At twenty-two, he'd emigrated —
In Montreal he was located;
And he was at the Great Lakes too

Dispatching parties by canoe
With voyageurs among the crew.

As more canoes like his departed
The northwest fur trade really started;
And in exchange for furs would come
Gunpowder, silver, cloth and rum.

Then as the fur trade grew and grew,
The canny merchants prospered too:
The warehouses on Rue Saint-Paul
Held James's wealth in Montreal.

When, angered by the Quebec Act,
America with troops attacked,
McGill and others made a pact
So Montreal would not be sacked.
Surrender was negotiated
And those invaders were placated.

Though Montreal was occupied,
James would not join the rebel side
And even voiced his detestation
Of this attempt at 'Liberation'.
To show McGill he was mistaken,
His cellar full of rum was taken.

When finally the armies went,
Benjamin Franklin then was sent
With revolutionary intent,
But found that none would heed his call

In French or English Montreal.
His journal, though, is with us yet:
It's called the Montreal Gazette.

The city prospered — James did too.
His civic reputation grew
And several times a seat he earned
When the Assembly was returned.
But he was not, for all his zest,
Deficient in self-interest.

In fact McGill was most adroit
Acquiring land around Detroit.
When that became a U.S. city,
He may have thought it was a pity,
But he obtained, by obligation,
Canadian lands in compensation.

That made him see it could be grand
To start to speculate in land.
Such enterprises made McGill,
Already wealthy, richer still,
And prompted him to make a will.

With gifts of money and of land
A University he planned,
Where many a future generation
Has owed to him their education;
And there Canadians honour still
The famous name of James McGill.

*John Graves Simcoe*
*Founder: Toronto*

# JOHN GRAVES SIMCOE
## (1752 – 1806)

*After a successful military career, John Graves Simcoe was
appointed the first Lieutenant Governor of the new province of
Upper Canada in 1791. His enthusiastic plans met with some
success and some disappointments, but they helped to found what
is now Ontario, where Simcoe Day is annually celebrated.*

All those who study Simcoe's story
Know he was very much a Tory.
He thought colonial solutions
Meant founding British institutions.
The land would flower with their insertion:
Democracy was pure subversion!

He named one river Thames, and he
Said there the capital should be.
He called it London, and would make
A road to link it to the Lake.

But people very soon would find
The Governor had changed his mind.
He said: "As capital, I aim
To grant instead Toronto's claim,
And henceforth York will be its name."

Said Joseph Brant, the Mohawk Chief:
"The Governor, in my belief,

All round our land has left his trace –
He's changed the name of every place!"

But Simcoe's main preoccupation
Was to enlarge the population.
Appeals for settlers were extensive;
The land they got was not expensive.

Whole townships too the Governor granted
To get the people firmly planted.
The eager methods that he used
Meant sometimes titles got confused.
He wheeled and dealed at such a rate
He could have thrived in Real Estate!

The many projects that he planned
To help enrich this vast new land
Were well-intentioned, great and grand –
But Britain didn't understand:
His masters didn't think it funny
If they were asked to send him money!

But using soldiers, he succeeded,
Built the roads the country needed,
And as was always his intention
Beat back U.S. intervention.

He started building Government House
Which definitely pleased his spouse:
His wife Elizabeth's pretensions

Were socially of huge dimensions,
And though the mansion was deferred
Elizabeth was not deterred.
Her High Society events
Were held instead in giant tents.

She played the Grande Dame with finesse
At balls where guests in sumptuous dress
Would gladly dance the night away
While stately orchestras would play.

When John Graves Simcoe had departed
His colony was truly started.
His name is in towns, lakes and streets,
And though he suffered some defeats
His zeal and eager dedication
Helped found the new Canadian nation.

# GEORGE VANCOUVER
## (1757 – 1798)

*George Vancouver's first voyages were with Captain Cook,*
*but he is most celebrated for his epic four-and-a-half year journey*
*along the western coast of Canada and the USA, charting over*
*seventy thousand miles of coastline.*

George Vancouver took a trip
At fourteen, on a naval ship.
His native England he forsook
To see the world with Captain Cook.
From him he was to learn the arts
Of making perfect maps and charts.

Cook's second trip with George aboard
The northwest coastal shores explored,
And George Vancouver was, what's more,
First European upon that shore.

Then off Cook went, two thousand miles,
To what he called the Sandwich Isles.
It's really hard to know just why he
Ignored their proper name, Hawaii.

The islanders thought Cook no friend,
And at their hands he met his end.
They nearly killed Vancouver too,
But he escaped with all his crew.

His death then would have been a pity —
For what would we have called the city?
But George lived on, and got promotion,
And sailed for the Pacific Ocean.
There, Spain was causing a commotion:
The coast was theirs, they had a notion.

The British government was furious,
Maintaining that the claim was spurious.
(The people living there, it's true,
Were never asked to give their view.)

Then José Martinez's band
Seized lots of British ships and land,
And when he dared to shout "Olé!"
The British cried: "No way, José!"

They needed now a speedy mover,
And so they sent in George Vancouver.
For what the British wanted most
Were surveys, up and down the coast.
"With those," they said, "you can declare
If there's a Northwest Passage there."

Some thought not all the coast was dry land —
Perhaps Alaska was an island?
George may have thought such views ridiculous,
But still, his survey was meticulous,
And all his skill and strength he put

Into that mapping, foot by foot.
The narrowest inlets he'd explore
In open boats, to reach the shore.

His survey, he could really boast,
Scanned sixty thousand miles of coast.
The small boats' trips increased the score
By something like ten thousand more.

Four years it took to bring it off —
Then, near the Isle of Baranof
Far to the north, Vancouver anchored
And took the rest for which he hankered.

"We've done it!" was his declaration,
"Get out the grog, in celebration!
And while we have our drinking session
Let's say farewell to one obsession,
The Northwest Passage! We have let it
Rule all our lives, and hope we met it.
Now we can simply say, 'FORGET IT!'
You might as well, to get to China,
Dig out a trench from Carolina."

Was he much wiser than he knew?
Digging a trench is what they'd do.
Southwards, years later, they installed it —
The Panama Canal they called it.

# SIR ALEXANDER MACKENZIE
## (1764 – 1820)

*Alexander Mackenzie was ten when his family emigrated
first to New York and then to Canada. He became a fur trader and
made two epic journeys west, trekking by canoe and on foot
in search of a route to the Pacific.*

The search for furs; this was the quest
Which led Mackenzie to the west.
For there, the wilderness was rife
With every kind of furry life:
Beavers and otters, foxes, minks,
The wolf, the marten and the lynx.

They all made fashionable furs
And classy headgear, His and Hers.
For then the fur trade went unchecked,
Though not politically correct.
Creatures were killed without apology,
And no one cared about ecology.

The Athabasca River ran
Beside the new Fort Chipewyan,
And here Mackenzie's trek began.
With just twelve men in three canoes,
Slave River was the route he'd choose.
Off to the west they paddled forth,

Then found the river heading north.

Mackenzie wouldn't be downcast:
They paddled on, and paddled fast.
One hundred miles a day they went,
To reach the ocean their intent.
When finally they saw the sea,
All frozen it appeared to be.

Mackenzie grumbled: "What a shame!
This river here by which we came,
Let Disappointment be its name."
But others thought that name too grim,
And later named it after him.

His colleagues in the trade, however,
Were not impressed by his endeavour.
They said: "A sea of ice won't suit
As any kind of trading route."
Mackenzie though was resolute,
And four years later, with nine men
And one dog, he set out again.

Peace River was the way to go,
But did they find it peaceful? No!
Mackenzie and his nine companions
Faced rapids and cascades and canyons,
Hauled the canoe and all their goods
Up rocky paths through gloomy woods;
Midst snowy mountains, never warm,

They camped, and sheltered from a storm.

Mackenzie took the chance to write
Of all they'd done until that night,
Then in an empty rum keg placed
His diary of the route they'd traced
And all the dangers they had faced.

He cast the keg into the river
And hoped his note it would deliver.
The postal service now is better —
Then, it was chancier... and wetter!

For weeks Mackenzie and his team
Went bravely struggling upstream,
And wondered, was it all a dream?
Perhaps, although they'd done their best,
There was no river to the West.

But then they met a local guide
Who led them to the Great Divide.
And west from here, they had a notion,
Lay the great Pacific Ocean.
But soon, by icy waters battered,
Their lone canoe was nearly shattered:
Instead of paddling, as they planned,
They had to journey overland.

They found a river, guides who knew
This land where giant cedars grew,

And villages where they would dine
On salmon, deer, and porcupine.

But further on, the records tell us,
They met the warlike Bella Bellas
And found them much less friendly fellas.

An angry warrior climbed aboard
And grabbed Mackenzie's gun and sword,
And said white men, a few weeks back,
Had used such weapons to attack.
(The story that he told was true:
It was Vancouver and his crew.)

Back in his own canoe once more,
"Follow!" they heard the warrior roar.
Instead, they raced towards the shore;
They climbed a rock, and on the top
There for the night they had to stop.

Next day, as soon as it was light,
Two war canoes came into sight:
The outlook wasn't very bright.
And yet Mackenzie showed no fear —
He said: "Before we disappear,
The world must know that I was here!"

He wrote a record of his visit —
Like Kilroy, only more explicit:
Upon the rock, in letters great,

He scrawled his own name, and the date.
He wrote too, so they'd understand,
He'd come from Canada, by land.

The others neither groused nor brooded
To see their names were not included,
For they were more concerned that day
With how to make their getaway.

The warriors' canoes gave chase
But finally they lost the race;
Yet still Mackenzie had to face
The cruel journey back to base.
Somehow, the party made their way
At nearly forty miles a day,
And Alexander gained much glory
By later publishing his story.

Among the readers, for a start,
There was Napoleon Bonaparte:
He planned to beat the British back
With a Canadian attack.

Back home, the King did not demur,
But promptly dubbed Mackenzie "Sir".
Which shows what marvels can occur
From starting out to search for fur!

# LAURA SECORD
## (1775-1868)

*In the War of 1812, Laura Secord made an epic solo trek to warn the*
*troops at Beaver Dams of a coming attack. Public recognition and*
*reward were a long time coming, but she finally got her deserved*
*fame, as well as her name on monuments and chocolate boxes.*

In history, the name of Laura
Has come to have a certain aura,
Although it's true that no one now
Remembers what they called her cow.

In 1812 the Yankees, sore
At Canada, began a war.
The Secords, on the British side,
Found that their home was occupied.
The U.S. officers with pride,
Declaring they would soon be winners,
Told Laura she must cook their dinners.

What could she do? There in her house
She watched the officers carouse.
She listened too, as they began
To boast about their battle plan.
They said, "These troops of Uncle Sam's
Will wipe them out at Beaver Dams!"

So Laura thought, "I must give warning!"
Before the sun rose in the morning
She slipped away, quite undetected,
To say attack should be expected.

The day dawned and the hot sun shone
But Laura just walked on and on
Through undergrowth and hidden by-ways
Avoiding checkpoints, roads and highways.

She waded many a stream and river
Her urgent message to deliver,
And found her courage sorely tested
In treacherous swamps, by snakes infested.
And some accounts will tell you how
By clinging to a passing cow
She managed with this bovine aid
The soldiers' capture to evade.

She reached Niagara, and she paled:
How could that craggy cliff be scaled?
But Laura's courage never failed.
She climbed and clung and didn't stop
Until she'd reached the very top.

With darkness falling all around her,
A group of Mohawk warriors found her.
With wonder and concern they scanned her,
And brought her to the post's commander.

"Well, you deserve," said James FitzGibbon,
"A campaign medal and a ribbon.
I'll send the Mohawks on their track
And mount a great surprise attack!"

His victory hopes were not mistaken -
Five hundred prisoners were taken;
And everyone admired the way
That Laura Secord saved the day.

In spite of her courageous mission
Poor Laura got no recognition.
She sent out many a petition
In which she always chanced to mention
It would be nice to get a pension.

When more than forty years had passed
Her deed was recognized at last.
The Prince of Wales, the future King,
Just happened to be visiting
And made, among his many calls,
A visit to Niagara Falls.

Here it was brought to his attention
That Laura merited a pension.
He sent one hundred pounds all told;
Laura, now eighty-six years old,
Declared: "Well, better late than never!
At least my name will live for ever."

And when she died, her name was praised
And several monuments were raised.
In 1913, Frank O'Connor
Said, "Laura's name I'd like to honour.
She lived life well, and took the knocks -
I'll put her on my chocolate box!
Her portrait will be fine and dandy
Paraded on my luscious candy."

So Laura's name has never perished
Wherever chocolate is cherished.

# SIR JOHN FRANKLIN
## (1786 – 1847)

*John Franklin was a naval officer who charted thousands of miles*
*of Canada's Arctic coast in the quest for the Northwest Passage.*
*He made four expeditions and met his death during the last one.*

King William Island's frozen ground
Was where John Franklin's corpse was found,
His bones the only indication
Of that brave life of exploration.

From age fourteen, his naval life
Was filled with roving and with strife.
Then, Franklin saw his true vocation
In Canadian exploration.

The powers-that-be were all obsessed
With finding routes from east to west.
They sought the Northwest Passage which
Would help make everybody rich.

Franklin's first journey had no luck:
In polar ice they nearly stuck.
The second time from Hudson Bay
To Yellowknife he made his way,
Then down the river Coppermine —
The prospect, though, was far from fine.

# The mysterious disappearance of Sir John Franklin finally explained...

Sometimes a frozen lake they crossed,
Their faces bitten by the frost.
Canoes on pairs of sleds were put:
Dogs dragged them, while men walked on foot.
The ice was honeycombed by rain,
And jagged edges caused great pain.
The men's and dogs' feet, when they bled,
Left on the ice a trail of red.

The journey seemed to take them ages,
And Franklin fumed with frequent rages.
No wonder that the Inuit feared
This sullen group, and disappeared.
And so, without the Inuits' aid,
The two canoes their journey made,
And for a month the coast surveyed.

Then food got short, and tempers too,
And murmurs of rebellion grew.
It wasn't long before John Franklin
Sensed grudges and resentments ranklin'.
He said: "We must return, it's plain:
I'll name this Point here Turnagain."
The men said: "Call it what you like —
But turn around, or we shall strike!"

They had no food, and their canoes
Were damaged far too much to use.
So overland the route they tried.
Frozen and starving, nine men died.

The rest, in order to survive,
Ate lichen just to keep alive.
A local tribe who knew the place
Found them, and brought them back to base.

Now, Franklin was a famous name;
And though a hero he became,
He found that life at home was boring,
And yearned again to go exploring.
Better equipped, he mapped once more
Hundreds of miles of Arctic shore.

Then late in life he got the chance
To make the final great advance.

Three hundred miles remained uncharted:
So for the Arctic coast he started —
But not before he watched them stowing
Three years' supplies to keep them going.
Steam boilers drove propellers, too,
And heated pipes to warm the crew.
A library of books was there,
And wine, cut-glass, and silverware.

In 1845, in May,
The ships sailed out to Baffin Bay.
But no one knew what happened then
To Franklin and his ships and men.
In that white world, so wild and weird,
They had completely disappeared.

The years passed — forty expeditions
Went sailing out on searching missions.
And Franklin's widow did her best
To press for yet another quest.
When she had waited fourteen years,
A gruesome find confirmed her fears.

King William Island was the site
Where Franklin's body came to light:
Two skeletons, one his, they guessed
From silver spoons that bore his crest.

The Northwest Passage now was mapped,
And in its icy wastes were trapped
Many explorers' ships and crews
Whose families had received no news
Of how they suffered and they died,
Unknown and unidentified.

At least they found John Franklin's grave —
A stern explorer, rash and brave:
For charts and maps his life he gave.

Though Europeans' success was heady,
The Inuit knew that coast already;
If Franklin with his dedication
Had sought out their co-operation,
He might have saved the situation.

# SAMUEL CUNARD
## (1787 - 1865)

*Born and brought up in Halifax, Nova Scotia, Samuel Cunard*
*joined his father's shipping company and pioneered the use of*
*steamships on the transatlantic route. The Cunard Line grew to be*
*one of the most prestigious operators of liners, famous for their*
*speed, luxury and reliability.*

A boy in Halifax would stay
Upon the docks and gaze all day
At sailing ships of every sort
Coming and going in the port.
Samuel Cunard had dreams that he
Would own a shipping company.

His father, a carpenter, saved hard
And bought a mail-boat - soon Cunard
Became indeed a noted name
Destined for even greater fame.

One day in England, Sam was on
The steam train built by Stephenson.
He came home with a novel notion:
Steam could take ships across the ocean!

In Boston, where he looked for cash,
The merchants said, "It's much too rash.
Such foolish schemes are sure to fail,

For Steam will never conquer Sail."

The British though were not so nervous:
They planned a transatlantic service
To carry mail by using steam,
And so they welcomed Samuel's scheme.

Britannia  was Cunard's first ship
To make the transatlantic trip.
Sixty-three passengers set sail
As well as copious bags of mail.
Samuel Cunard was there on board
To hear the dockside crowds who roared.
The Captain shouted orders through
A speaking trumpet to the crew.
The steam the engines would provide
Drove giant paddles, either side.

Among the crew there were three cats
To deal with mailbag-eating rats.
A cow too in a padded stall
Would yield fresh milk for one and all.
The passengers at meals might dine
On pea soup, fish pie, meat and wine,
And breakfast could be steak with hock,
For drinks were served from six o'clock.

When the ship rolled, the sea would slosh
Downstairs, and make the rooms awash.
For sea-sick people, stewards kept handy

Glasses of water mixed with brandy.

But in twelve days Britannia  came
To Halifax, with great acclaim.
And on to Boston then she sailed
Where as a hero Sam was hailed.
With banquets and a big parade
Great tribute to Cunard was paid.
Soon he was undisputed king
Of transatlantic travelling.

The Admiralty then made a move
Of which Cunard did not approve.
His ships were requisitioned for
The troops of the Crimean War,
And many journeys then they made
With horses for the Light Brigade.

And wounded soldiers too were brought
Across the Black Sea to the port
Where skillful nursing was provided,
And Florence Nightingale presided.

After the War, the north Atlantic
Saw other battles no less frantic,
For U.S. lines were fighting hard
To wrest the laurels from Cunard.

The Collins Line pulled out all stops
With private bathrooms, barber shops,

Deep carpets and electric bells
And brass spittoons too, shaped like shells.

Cunard's speed records they must beat
To make their victory complete.
The Collins Line achieved success
By crossing in ten days or less.

Cunard competed to eclipse
Its rivals with new, bigger ships -
But Samuel always stressed the need
To favour safety over speed.

The Collins Line, which took more chances,
Wrecked ships, and wrecked its own finances.
Eventually the Line was gone,
But sturdily Cunard sailed on.

Sam died in 1865;
His liners kept his name alive.
Cunard's esteem would never vary:
The Queens, Elizabeth and Mary,
The QE2, Cunard Princess,
Continued to ensure success.

And all that power and esteem
Came from young Samuel's boyhood dream
Watching the ships sail to and fro
In Halifax, so long ago.

# WILLIAM LYON MACKENZIE
## (1795 – 1861)

*A journalist and a politician, Mackenzie was a tireless and fierce
advocate of reform. As a member of Upper Canada's Assembly,
he was expelled and re-elected many times, and became the first
mayor of Toronto. In 1837 he led an unsuccessful rebellion,
fled to the U.S.A,, was jailed, and then returned after an amnesty
to further turbulent years in Canadian politics.*

The mind of William Lyon Mackenzie
Was in a state of constant frenzy.
When Tory values were the norm,
He preached political reform.

He started, to promote his aims,
Papers with many different names.
When one would fail, he wasn't vexed:
He'd bounce right back and start the next.

In Upper Canada's Assembly
Mackenzie's foes were all a-trembly.
He lashed the opposition ranks
And even criticised the Banks —
An attitude, which some might say,
Would also find support today...

He was elected, then rejected,
And then once more was re-elected.

In such esteem the people held him
That when his enemies expelled him
A crowd of several hundred went
And marched right into Parliament.
And after that the by-election
Made him the popular selection.

Then Yonge Street rang with cheers of praise,
As bagpipes and a hundred sleighs
Went in a great procession, led
By William, riding at the head.

Yet still his foes, infuriated,
Kept booting out the man they hated —
But he was always re-instated.
He said: "If this goes on much more,
I'll ask for a revolving door!"

Now when Toronto first was founded,
Up to new heights Mackenzie bounded.
The brand new Council then and there
Made William Lyon Mackenzie mayor.
But in provincial politics
He couldn't beat the Governor's tricks:
That ruling agent of the Crown
Kept putting the reformers down.

Mackenzie now began devising
A plan to stage an armed uprising.
He wrote, to fuel the demonstration,

An Independence Declaration,
And made, to gather his supporters,
Montgomery's Tavern his headquarters.
They prepared to sally forth, "Best
Take Toronto from the west."

Thursday was meant to be the day
When they would all be on their way,
But someone gave the city warning
And so they marched on Tuesday morning.
Then by the Guards with bullets spattered,
Mackenzie's rebel army scattered.

Though further reinforcements then
Came to increase Mackenzie's men,
The city's soldiers came to meet them
And swiftly managed to defeat them.

Mackenzie fled, the battle lost —
Niagara's River then he crossed,
And soon on Navy Island there
Americans arrived to share
As volunteers, with his persuasion,
A plan for Canada's invasion.

They were bombarded from the bank
And then their main supply ship sank,
And soon the U.S. Government
Decided it was time they went.

For William, prosecution waited:
Neutrality he'd violated.
Released on bail, not beaten yet,
He started up a new Gazette,
And wrote, with somewhat rash intent,
Attacks upon the President.

Jailed for a year, he then was pardoned,
And soon his attitudes had hardened.
Back home in Canada once more,
A lot of things made William sore.
He lashed old colleagues, and old laws —
A rebel upon every cause.
He was a man of great panache,
Eccentric, maverick and rash.

Our parties might have more appeal
With some of his reforming zeal.

# DR. JAMES BARRY
## (1795-1865)

*James Barry was an army surgeon who rose to high rank and was put in charge of all Canada's military hospitals. When he died it was discovered that Dr. Barry was a woman.*

No woman could be asked to marry
The famous surgeon called James Barry.
He'd have to stay upon the shelf,
For he was that same sex himself.

She played a man not from perversity,
But just to get to university.
In Edinburgh she - or he -
Obtained a medical degree.
Then she began within a year
An army medical career.

And soon she thought, "What I deserve is
A spell in the Colonial Service."
So her career began to burgeon
In Cape Town, as Assistant Surgeon,
And once when typhus there was rife
She even saved the Governor's life.

Her temper, though, was quite a scandal -
She often flew right off the handle.

Her macho image she would fuel
Sometimes, by fighting in a duel.

Her ghost, the Cape Town legends say,
Still haunts a glen beside a bay.

Her brilliance was duly noted
And she was constantly promoted.
She reached the height of army fame
When out to Canada she came.
The hospitals both small and large
Were all in Dr. Barry's charge.
In army ranks she caused some storms
By pushing through a few reforms.

"Separate quarters," said James Barry,
"Should be the right of men who marry -
And what is more, the soldiers' diet
Is dull enough to cause disquiet.
They'll find a roast a great relief
From eating nothing but boiled beef.

Now, those straw pillows on each bed -
Put feathers in them all instead.
Water and drains too, need improving.
Well, don't just stand and stare - get moving!"

The thankful soldiers soon began
To say, "James Barry - he's our man!"

The doctor relished ostentation -
In fact she caused a great sensation:
Through Montreal she made her way
In fur coat, in a scarlet sleigh,
A black manservant at her side
With a small dog, her pet and pride.

The secret she had kept concealed,
After her death was soon revealed.
The powers-that-be made quite a fuss -
They cried, "She made a fool of us!
A woman surgeon, in the army -
The very notion drives us barmy!"

Such things were quite beyond their ken:
She'd taken on the world of men
And shown, the only way she could,
That women could be just as good.
She really opened up their eyes,
This feminist, in male disguise.

# SIR JOHN A. MACDONALD
## (1815 – 1891)

*John Macdonald began his career as a lawyer in Kingston, Ontario,
then entered politics, becoming the leader of the Conservatives
and in 1867 the first Prime Minister of the new
federal Canadian nation.*

John was, at twenty-one, a star –
The judges called him to the Bar.

Though soon, by some opponents' reckoning,
Bars of another kind were beckoning,
John thrived in party politics
And quickly mastered all the tricks.
Premier by 1856,
He saw that only Federation
Could forge a new Canadian nation.

So in Quebec the delegations
Began, some with persistent patience,
Others with fiery protestations,
To try to find a joint solution
And hammer out a constitution.

Eighteen days talking it would need
To get the document agreed.
So after many a deal, and dance,
Confederation got its chance.

It finally became a fact
When Britain opted to enact
The British North American Act.

Then politicians must debate
How to describe this latest state.
A Kingdom? Oh dear, no – because
A Kingdom's just what Britian was.

New Brunswick Premier Leonard Tilley
Believed such nit-picking was silly.
He said: "The Psalms, in my opinion,
Suggest we use the name Dominion,
For one of them declares that "He
Dominion shall have from sea to sea."

They all agreed upon the name;
John A. Macdonald then became
The first Prime Minister to stand
As leader of this great new land.

He did indeed think it should be
A land that stretched from sea to sea,
And so, to realize the dream
He backed a most audacious scheme
To build a grandiose creation;
A Railroad that would span the nation.

He thought that, as in all his deals,
Some patronage would oil the wheels.

Hugh Allen and his syndicate
Would think a railroad contract great
And Allen made most generous offers
To swell Macdonald's party coffers.

The syndicate would be selected
When John Macdonald was elected –
But there was something he neglected:
Surprise, surprise – he never thought
To tell the people he'd been bought!

But soon the Liberals told the world
And what a scandal then unfurled.
His reputation undermined,
Sir John reluctantly resigned.

But five years later, he was back –
The railroad plan was back on track.
This stunning engineering feat
In only four years was complete.

And soon it carried troops to quell
The second rising of Riel.
Macdonald chose a rash solution
And authorized his execution.
The anger and recrimination
Threatened once more to split the nation.

Somehow the Grand Old Man survived
And in the next election thrived.

He died, still in the driving seat,
His colourful career complete.
He had well earned his reputation
As Father of Confederation.

# CHARLES BLONDIN
## (1824 – 1897)

*Blondin was from a circus family and became world-famous
for his spectacular stunts, particularly his tightrope walks
across Niagara Falls.*

Blondin, soon after he could talk,
Was learning how to tightrope-walk.
His father knew what he was at:
He was a famous acrobat.

So Blondin felt the great delights
Of prancing round at heady heights.
One day he cried: "Adventure calls —
I'll walk across Niagara Falls!"
And so in l859,
Blondin prepared to toe the line.

The foaming river stretched out wide —
One thousand feet from side to side.
One slip, and plunging he would go
Into the torrent down below.

The crowd gasped as he took his pole
And started for his distant goal,
With dainty steps, precise and slow,
And not a trace of vertigo.

In twenty minutes, and no more,
He stepped upon the further shore.
The cheering and the shouting drowned
Even the gushing water's sound.

He'd crossed the Falls, and didn't drop —
And after that he wouldn't stop.
Each time he saw a chance, he'd grab it:
He simply couldn't kick the habit.

Blindfold he crossed, straight as an arrow;
Then on the rope he wheeled a barrow.
He crossed with someone on his back,
And with his feet inside a sack.

And then he took a stove along
And watched by the admiring throng
He cooked an omelette in mid-air
And calmly ate it, then and there.
He savoured it, and didn't gobble,
And never made a single wobble.

Through all his great Niagara stunts,
He never put a foot wrong once.
He did things no one else would try,
And just kept walking — high, and dry.
Though people thought he'd soon be dead,
He died at seventy-three — in bed.

# SIR SANDFORD FLEMING
## (1827 – 1915)

*As a railway engineer, Sandford Fleming helped to build the new railroads across Canada. He invented the international system of Time Zones still used today.*

Many good results are stemming
From the work of Sandford Fleming:
Railways, time zones, maps and charts,
Aid for science and the arts,
Progress all across the land
Was helped by Fleming's guiding hand.

An engineer and a surveyor,
He soon became a major player
Among the ranks of those who pressed
For a railroad east to west.

In Newfoundland, and on the plains,
He planned the tracks to take the trains.
Up in the Rockies fierce disputes
Flared up about the likely routes,
But Fleming was a pioneer
Who liked to get his way, it's clear —
And, well — he was Chief Engineer!

Soon, trains across the land would hurry —

But Sandford Fleming had a worry.
He'd rush to catch a train, and miss it,
And curse in language most explicit;
With rage he made his protests vocal:
"The time we keep is too damned local!"

For way back then, each township said:
"At noon, the sun's straight overhead."
So when Quebec said: "It's noon, pronto!"
"Eleven-thirty!" said Toronto.
This caused rail travellers some vexation,
Changing their watches at each station.

So Fleming then said: "How sublime
If we could have a Standard Time.
A twenty-four hour clock we need,
Which even idiots can read.
The world we should divide, what's more,
In Time Zones, making twenty-four.
On every clock, one time is shown
Until you reach another zone."

Both here and in the U.S.A.
The railway managers said: "Hey!
We do believe you've shown the way."

But others said that Fleming's scheme
Was just another crackpot's dream;
And some declared his plans so flighty
They even flouted God Almighty.
These zealots never stopped condemning

The sinful ways of Sandford Fleming.

It took some years of arguments
Till scientists and governments
Agreed that Fleming's plan made sense.
In 1884 they opted
For Standard Time to be adopted.
So Fleming was triumphant then —
And never missed a train again.

That wasn't all, by any means:
He was the Chancellor of Queen's,
And back in 1851,
When postage stamps were first begun,
He drew the first Canadian one.

He helped to make Canadians able
To reach Australia by cable,
And when he'd nothing else to do
He even wrote a prayer book too.

No wonder people were delighted
When he, aged seventy, was knighted.
Perhaps when honoured by the Queen
She asked the time, and he was seen
To say: "Which Time Zone do you mean?"

A nod to Fleming is a must
For travellers, however fussed,
Each time their watches they adjust.

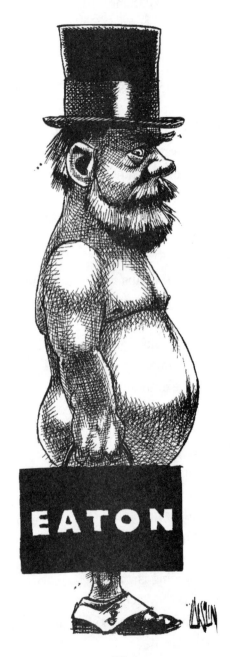

EATON

# TIMOTHY EATON
## (1834-1907)

*Timothy Eaton founded the first of the Eaton chain of stores
in Toronto in 1869, and his commercial ideas revolutionized
shopping in Canada.*

From Ireland to Canadian shores
To found a famous chain of stores
Came Timothy Eaton, now renowned
Wherever shoppers can be found.

Shopping was ripe for revolution
On Eaton had his own  solution;
And so in 1869
The first store in the Eaton line
At Yonge Street started operation
And caused at once a big sensation.

Eaton began with great panache,
Declaring: "We take only cash.
The barter system, we have shed it -
What's more, you needn't ask for credit,
Because you just ain't gonna geddit!

Don't seek to bargain, for we  won't -
You pay our fixed price, or you don't.
We offer value and fair play -

That's retailing, the Eaton way!"

But one more promise Eaton made
Really amazed the retail trade:
He said, "We'll give back what you paid
If you are not quite satisfied
With any product we supplied."

His rivals scoffed, and said disaster
Would come within a year, or faster.
But Timothy soon proved them wrong
As shoppers to his store did throng.

And what was even more surprising,
He wanted honest  advertising -
Insisting, "Everything must be
Exactly what we guarantee.
No lies and no exaggeration
Must mar the Eaton reputation."

He made more innovations later -
Even installed an elevator.
When customers at first were wary
He tried to show it wasn't scary:
Wax figures then were put inside
And up and down were seen to ride -
A ruse that was a bit surprising
From one who liked true advertising.

Now as the Eaton empire grew

He pioneered mail-order too.
His catalogue was justly famed:
The Prairie Bible  it was named.

While Eaton's name grew more prestigious
The founder still remained religious.
He hated liquor, wouldn't let
His stores sell any cigarette.
At home, nobody had the chance
To play a game of cards, or dance.

At work, he was paternalist -
A fervent anti-unionist.
His workers even were afraid
To watch the Labour Day parade.

And yet, unlike the rest, he'd fix
For Eaton's stores to close at six;
And afternoons on Saturday
He said should be a holiday.

His methods prospered - soon he'd boast
A chain of stores from coast to coast.
Then, with the founding father gone,
His sons and grandsons carried on.

# CALIXA LAVALLÉE
## (1842 – 1891)

*Calixa Lavallée grew up in a musical family, and became
a celebrated performer, as well as the composer of
Canada's national anthem.*

Calixa was a gifted boy —
He was his parents' pride and joy.
His father taught him all he knew:
The violin, and organ too.
His piano-playing was first-rate —
And all this, by the age of eight!

And when he moved to Montreal
His playing really stunned them all.
And then, still in his early teens,
He took a trip to New Orleans
And there he won a competition.
He met another star musician
And off on tour the pair did go
Down to Brazil and Mexico.

This roving life he found so grand,
He joined the Union Army Band,
And got a wound, in Maryland.

He lived in Boston for a spell

And taught there, and performed as well.
He even wrote an opera too,
Which had the title T.I.Q.
He said it meant The Indian Question.
To settle it, was his suggestion.
To think his music might achieve
That end was just a bit naïve.

Then back in Canada once more,
A great occasion lay in store:
A Governor-General's installation
Required a musical sensation.
Lavallée was the man they chose
A fine cantata to compose.

He trained a choir with soloists
And many instrumentalists.
The show was lavish and expensive,
The praise was fervent and extensive.

Calixa, though, near lost his senses:
They wouldn't pay him his expenses!

He got the chance, though, one year later
For a performance even greater.
The Société St. Jean-Baptiste
Was holding a gigantic feast:
To celebrate, was their intention,
A French-Canadian convention.

They said: "We need a national song:
With Lavallée, we can't go wrong.
So with O Canada we'll show 'em —
Look up the words now, of the poem.
Calixa said: "No need — I know 'em."

He had it finished very soon,
And so was born the national tune.
A massive choir three thousand strong
Gave voice to the composer's song;
Three bands were playing, and the crowd
All clapped and cheered it long and loud.

And soon at every hall and stage
O Canada was all the rage.
It topped, whenever it was played,
The 1880's Hit Parade.
And then it wasn't very long
Before the nation knew the song.

Wherever it is sung today,
Canadians here or far away
Honour Calixa Lavallée:
O Canada is here to stay.

# WILLIAM CORNELIUS VAN HORNE
## (1843- 1915)

*Van Horne was a genius of the railroad, and when he became
general manager of the Canadian Pacific in 1882, his powerful
personality and organizing skills were able to get the
coast-to-coast railway completed in record time.*

In 1843 was born
William Cornelius Van Horne.
At just fourteen, the bright young boy
Got railroad work in Illinois,
Rose in the ranks, and shortly knew
Each railroad job there was to do.

Canadians said, "Now here's a star:
We'll let him run the C.P.R.!"
And so Van Horne began with zest
To build a railroad to the West.

In Winnipeg he made his base:
It was a booming, bustling place
Where real estate's great fluctuation
Depended on the speculation:
"Where will they put the railroad station?"

This happened all along the line
As people hankered for a sign
Of where the stops would be located -

For there the prices escalated.
Whole towns grew up, and their position
Depended on Van Horne's decision.

In the Canadian Pacific
Some thought him great, and some horrific.
His nickname had a certain sting:
They called him Boss of Everything -
And anyone who answered back
Was sure to find he'd got the sack.
Indeed he ruled the C.P.R.
Just like a fierce, despotic Czar.

And yet in most of those he hired
A fervent loyalty he inspired.
Using his methods, crews could lay
Up to four miles of track a day,
And he himself went out and back
To check the current End of Track.

When on these trips he often might
Play poker with the men all night
And then, such were his staying powers
Van Horne would work for fourteen hours.

To everybody's admiration
He still had time for recreation -
Collected fossils, drew cartoons
And on his violin played tunes;
Practical jokes he liked to do,

And he was fond of gardening too.

Asked where his powers had their source
He said, "From food and drink of course.
I eat and drink all that I can
And smoke as much as any man!"

The rails pushed on across the prairie
And made the tribes who roamed there wary.
They saw their hunting grounds cut back
By settlements along the track.

The Rockies shortly would be reached
But where would that stark range be breached?
Van Horne chose a disputed course:
He'd use the Pass at Kicking Horse.

Some said he never could complete
That dangerous and daring feat.
Thousands upon those peaks did swarm
Confronting avalanche and storm,
Dangled by ropes to cut and hack
The dizzy ledge to hold the track.
Rocks blasted out by dynamite
Sped forth like cannon-balls in flight.
Men tumbled from the precipice
And fell into the deep abyss.
Tall bridges, out of timber made,
Across the canyons swung and swayed.

In squalid camps the men survived
While secret whisky peddlers thrived.
The stuff was cutely smuggled in
Sometimes in bibles made of tin,
In eggs, and loco boilers too -
And once an organ held the brew.

Van Horne would come to see the work:
There was no danger he would shirk.
Walking for miles, great risks he'd take,
And fell once in an icy lake.

And all the while, he took great chances
To save the C.P.R.'s finances,
Put his own money in the stock
And claimed it was as firm as rock.
And when things got into a fix
He even played at politics,
Supplying a luxurious train
To help supporters to campaign.

When Van Horne to the west coast came
He chose Vancouver's site, and name.
Back east his powers still didn't lapse:
Somehow he filled the final gaps.
For years he'd kept the plans alive,
And got them done in less than five.

And now, as highest praise was given,
The very Last Spike could be driven.

At Craigellachie, in B.C.,
There gathered many a V.I.P.,
And happily they cheered and clamoured
To see, at last, the Last Spike hammered.

Van Horne, who must have felt relief
As well as pride, was very brief:
"Now this is all that I can say:
The work's well done in every way."
The bearded and top-hatted crowd
All cheered and clapped him long and loud.

Van Horne's amazing operation
Had forged the rails that spanned a nation.
He'd built two thousand miles of track,
And yet Van Horne could not sit back.
A quarter century he spent
As chairman and as president
Ensuring people near and far
Knew all about the C.P.R.

The whole rail network, out of pride,
Stopped for five minutes when he died,
So that all Canada could mourn
William Cornelius Van Horne.

# LOUIS RIEL
## (1844-1885)

*Louis Riel led two rebellions trying to establish lands and rights
for the Métis, descendants of indigenous peoples and early
European settlers. His campaigns both peaceful and military, led
to the founding of Manitoba, but his eventual trial and execution
caused long-lasting and passionate controversy.*

The Métis, from two races grown,
Became a nation of their own.
To the Red River thousands went
And made a farming settlement,
And twice a year they all would go
To hunt the herds of buffalo.

This bright boy from the distant prairie
Went eastward to a seminary.
In Montreal his education
Earned him a dazzling reputation.
Mastering Math, French, Greek and Latin,
Louis topped every class he sat in.

And while the boy was educated
Four provinces were federated
To make what was, in their opinion,
A most spectacular Dominion.

Sir John Macdonald was Prime Minister.
The Métis didn't think him sinister;

But Canada approached one day
The Company called Hudson's Bay
And told them the Dominion planned
To buy out most of 'Rupert's Land'.
They said, "We fear a confrontation
Will lead to US annexation
Unless it's checked by our new nation."

Although the land was bought and sold
The people living there weren't told.
So when they saw surveyors there
Rebellion was in the air.
Louis, their chosen leader, went
To ask what these intruders meant.
"You have no rights here," said Riel.
(The less polite said, "Go to hell!")

The land surveyors then withdrew -
So did Macdonald's Governor too.
Fort Garry was the new H.Q.
And over it a new flag flew -
The Métis flag for all to see,
Resplendent with the fleur de lis.

Riel proclaimed a government
And was elected President.
Macdonald sent out Donald Smith
For Louis' men to parley with:
His promises were just a myth.
The Métis, thinking they were meant,

Believed that Canada's intent
Was totally benevolent.

And so they set their prisoners free,
But they abused their liberty.
Each called himself a Canada Firster:
As racists, there was no one worster.
They marched in fury on Fort Garry
But snowdrifts forced the troops to tarry
And so the expedition failed:
They were surrounded, caught and jailed.

Perhaps unwisely then, Riel
Called on their leader in his cell.
He was a man called Thomas Scott,
The angriest bigot of the lot.

He threatened he would kill Riel -
He beat the warder up as well.
For bearing arms against the state
Scott went on trial and learned his fate:
By firing squad his end he'd make.
It proved to be a big mistake:
Scott's standing up to then was zero,
But now he was Ontario's hero.

Macdonald wished the Métis nation
To join the growing Federation
So with a Métis delegation
He did a deal for integration.

Riel's dream province was a fact
Under the Manitoba Act.
Riel rejoiced, but in the end
Found John Macdonald was no friend.

The velvet glove, he'd understand,
Concealed a ruthless iron hand.
The force that claimed it came to police
Would never give the rebels peace.

And so Riel was forced to roam,
An exile from his own true home.
And though three times his people sent
Riel to sit in Parliament
The Government despite this call
Would not admit him there at all.
At last, "You're pardoned," they would say,
"Provided that you stay away."

The Métis, overwhelmed and fleeced
By settlers coming from the east,
By now had in large numbers gone
To live by the Saskatchewan.
From tribal ancestors they came,
And felt the land was theirs to claim.

Though Ottawa at length agreed,
It acted with such lack of speed
The Métis knew they must rebel -
And who could lead them but Riel?

And Louis welcomed the decision -
He had a messianic vision
That he was chosen now to be
The man to make his people free.

With meetings and a Bill of Rights
He tried to do it with no fights.
But secret forces then were sent
By John Macdonald's government
Which feared the Métis, wanting more,
Would spark a greater Civil War.

Only two Cree lent their might
To give support to Louis' fight.
And yet he found that he could meet
The soldiers, and inflict defeat.

Louis Riel's success in arms
Set off a series of alarms -
Macdonald said in some despair:
"We need to get troops quickly there."

The railroad's chief said, "We will chance it
If you in turn will just finance it!"
So, soon the railroad's gaps were filled,
The troops sent, many Métis killed -
Reduced, when ammunition fails,
To firing buttons, stones and nails.

The troops could no more be defied:

Riel surrendered and was tried.
He told the jury that his aim
Had always only been to claim
The land rights in his people's name:
But then the Guilty  verdict came.

The jury made a plea for mercy:
The Crown, ignoring controversy,
Hanged Louis - and by that ensured
A quarrel that has still endured.
Rebel or martyr? Though he's gone,
The argument still carries on.

Riel declared it made him sick
That Protestant and Catholic
Could not shake hands - he voiced his fears
That this could take two hundred years.

Progress has since been somewhat slow  -
Still, there's a century to go!

# CAPTAIN JOSHUA SLOCUM
## (1844 – 1909)

*Joshua Slocum grew up in Nova Scotia and went to sea at sixteen,
becoming a superb sailor and navigator. After many voyages he
made history as the first yachtsman to sail round the world solo.*

He was an ancient mariner
From a century ago
And Joshua Slocum was his name
A name the world would know.

He was the first to take a ship
With billowing sails unfurled
And sail it on a perilous trip
Alone around the world.

On Nova Scotia's wildest shores
A wild young boy was he
And as he grew, he quickly knew
He'd run away to sea.

As cook and mate and skipper
Around the globe he'd roam
Then with a wife begin a life
Upon a floating home.

He sailed the seas to many a land

From Rio to Hong Kong
And everywhere that Joshua sailed
Virginia came along.

She bore him several children
Each on a different yacht
And as they floated on their boat
She cooked and sewed and taught.

There were lessons every morning
And when she got the chance
She'd play the grand piano
And even sing and dance.

For thirteen years of marriage
They lived the sailing life;
Then she died, and two years later
Joshua took a second wife.

She tried the floating housewife's role
But she'd rather stay at home.
So Joshua said: "Then all alone
Around the world I'll roam."

In two years he had built a sloop
And it was called the Spray.
He stepped aboard in Boston
And he boldly sailed away.

Never had mariner before

Been seized with such a notion:
To face alone the great Unknown
Upon the restless ocean.

Through gales and fogs and storms he sailed
In lonely isolation.
He'd sing a tune, or with the Moon
He'd hold a conversation.

Harpooning turtles, shooting sharks,
He went his curious way,
And fried a dish of flying fish
Which landed on the Spray.

Atlantic waves, Pacific swells,
Like oxen he could yoke 'em.
No earthly force could stop the course
Of Captain Joshua Slocum!

He was at ease with V.I.P.'s
In each port he was at,
But in Cape Town, puzzled Kruger
Who thought the Earth was flat.

Once, lying ill with stomach cramps,
He said he saw appear
A ghost from the Columbus crew
Who took the helm to steer.

Not only storms were challenging

His navigator's arts.
A goat he'd taken on the boat
One day ate up the charts.

For nearly fifty thousand miles
And three years he did roam,
Then in his suit and black felt hat
He stepped ashore at home.

What seas he'd sailed, what sights he'd seen
From Sydney to Samoa.
His journey, many claimed, had been
The greatest trip since Noah!

# THE DONNELLYS  (d. 1880)

*The Donnelly family terrorized their local neighborhood
in Ontario for over twenty years of robbery, rustling and murder.
In 1880 James Carroll led a vigilante group against them,
intent on wholesale massacre. . .*

The Donnellys from Tipperary
Had habits that were really scary.
Johannah and her husband James
With ruthless violence made their names.

They and their seven sons would go
Round Lucan in Ontario
Like madmen roaring into battle.
They torched the barns and stole the cattle
And murdered travellers for cash.
Away on horseback they would dash
To revel, laugh and count their plunder.

It really isn't any wonder
That policemen who were posted there
Preferred to seek a job elsewhere.

And thus for over two decades
The feared Black Donnellys  made their raids.
But then James Carroll took a hand
And gathered up a vengeful band.

At dead of night, with blade and shot,
They tried to massacre the lot.
Although a few escaped and fled,
Most of the Donnellys were dead.

James Carroll to the court-house went;
Though some who saw that night's event
Described the murders they had spied,
"NOT GUILTY!" all the jury cried.

In spite of facts, there's few who'd say
That justice wasn't done that day.
Most people clearly shared the view
Declared by twelve good men and true.

The murdering Donnellys are gone
And yet their legend lingers on.
Some local people give their word
That ghostly hooves at night are heard.
I can believe it - maybe you  can:
The Donnellys still lurk in Lucan!

Believe It or Not!

ANNA SWAN STOOD 7'6"
IN HER BARE FEET WHILE
HANK SNOW STOOD A BIT
OVER 5!... BUT ONLY
WHEN HE WORE LIFTS
AND COWBOY BOOTS.

BOTH WERE FROM
NOVA SCOTIA!

# ANNA SWAN
## (1846 – 1888)

*Born and raised in Nova Scotia, Anna Swan found that her great height brought her fame and fortune in exhibitions, tours and circuses, as well as a husband of similar stature.*

Anna was born a normal size,
But gave her parents a surprise.
Of thirteen children, only she
Grew up so very speedily.
When she was five, though they stayed small,
Anna was nearly five feet tall.

Then P.T.Barnum – not a slow man
To seize his chances as a showman –
Saw Anna when she reached sixteen,
And said: "She'll wow the showbiz scene!
At seven feet six, and nothing less,
I'll call this stunning girl, I guess,
The Nova Scotia Giantess!
And she'll draw crowds to my Museum
Much bigger than the Coliseum."

Anna was not at all inhibited
By being so publicly exhibited.
Satin – one hundred yards or more –
Made up the costume that she wore.

Though people goggled at her height
She chatted to them with delight.

Besides her payment, which would be
A monthly thousand-dollar fee,
Barnum agreed that he would pay
A tutor for three hours a day;
And Anna learned to sing and play.

Anna was lucky to survive
A fire in 1865.
The building's windows were so small
That through them she could never crawl.
Museum workers smashed a wall
And rescued her, as flames did crackle
With pulley, rope, and block and tackle.

Travelling to Europe from the States
She met her husband, Martin Bates –
Shipboard romances can be lucky:
He was the Giant from Kentucky!
His height was seven feet three inches,
No problem when it came to clinches.

Married in London with euphoria,
They entertained for Queen Victoria.
Anna declared: "We will appear
On tour in Europe for a year.
The posters when we put them up'll
Announce:

## "WORLD'S LARGEST MARRIED COUPLE!"

They built on an Ohio farm
A house of most enormous charm:
Doors nine feet high no heads would catch,
And there was furniture to match.

A home for giants, His and Hers,
Just like a Dolls' House, in reverse –
A home to mark the huge success
Of Nova Scotia's Giantess!

# ALEXANDER GRAHAM BELL
## (1847 – 1922)

*Bell was born in Scotland and moved to Canada with his parents in
1870. His lifelong interest was teaching the deaf to speak, but he
was a brilliant inventor: a pioneer not only of the telephone, but of
sound recording, sonar detection, hydrofoils, and flying machines.*

Alexander Graham Bell,
His parents thought, was far from well.
So they decided they would go
To Brantford, in Ontario..
Once there, his health improved immensely,
And he began to work intensely.

Enthusiastically he'd teach
His father's system, Visible Speech.
The symbols, which were quite unique,
Could help the deaf to learn to speak.

And meanwhile Bell pursued with zest
Another scientific quest.
For it was one of his desires
To send speech by electric wires.
Thus he believed we could, one day,
Converse with people far away.

The telephone was in the offing —

Which didn't stop the people scoffing.
To make words carry, they'd no doubt
The only thing to do was shout!
And when they heard what Bell was after,
They simply doubled up with laughter.

But Bell and Watson, his assistant,
Remained courageous and persistent,
And in their workshop day and night
They toiled to prove that they were right.

Watson one night heard Bell's voice call —
It wasn't coming through the wall,
But down the wires, to Watson's ear:
"Please come here, Watson!" loud and clear.
Watson rushed in to tell his mentor:
"You sure are one great inventor!"

Bell got his patent applications
For his "electric undulations",
And very soon he got the chance
To make a really great advance.

From Tutela Heights his voice would go
To Paris, in Ontario.
And later, when he made a call
To greet his friends in Montreal,
They all cried, when they heard him speak:
"Le Téléphone — c'est magnifique!"

But then, big telegraphic firms
Boldly infringed the patent's terms;
To back his claim, Bell did resort
To lengthy battles through the court.

His company, Bell Telephone,
Was internationally known,
But Bell's resolve was unrelenting:
He just went on and on inventing.

He sent sound down a beam of light
And made experiments with flight,
Like an enormous man-powered kite;
And as these craft got off the ground,
Bell pioneered recorded sound.

Today, he would approve when shown
The wonders of the mobile phone —
But would he really wish to toast
The chatty radio phone-in host?

Or would he feel that each invention
Has some effects too brash to mention?
Such outcomes he could hardly know
Of that first call, so long ago,
At Brantford, in Ontario.

# EMMA ALBANI
## (1847 – 1930)

*Emma Albani from Montreal became an international opera star,*
*but still maintained her popularity at home, where she was*
*known as Canada's 'Queen of Song'.*

Just who was Marie Lajeunesse?
An operatic star, no less.
But when she sought the road to fame,
Like many stars, she changed her name:
EMMA ALBANI she became.

In childhood, she had learned the art:
Her teacher praised her from the start,
Where she grew up, in Montreal.
(He was her father, after all.)

They moved when she was seventeen
To Albany, a whole new scene:
That's why she later thought it witty
To take her stage name from that city.
The spelling, also rather wittily,
Made people think she came from Italy.

There, in the theatre at Messina,
She made her debut, as Amina:
La Sonnambula was her break —

The audience, though, stayed wide awake.

The same role made her all the rage
Upon the Covent Garden stage;
She then, with her career begun,
Married the theatre owner's son.
Apart from all his style and charm,
The move did her career no harm.

And there, for twenty years and more,
Her voice made audiences roar,
And cry out: "Bravo!" and "Encore!"

New Wagner operas she was in,
Like Tannhauser and Lohengrin.
She sang in New York, at the Met —
Just how prestigious can you get?
And there for Verdi, lucky fellow,
Albani premiered Otello.

Although on world-wide tours she'd roam,
She made her theme song Home Sweet Home.
And here at home, she was the toast
Of countless fans, from coast to coast.
With bands and fireworks,
crowds would throng
To hear the nation's 'Queen of Song'.

This pleased her most, although our star
Sang for the Kaiser and the Tsar,

And caused a lot of royal euphoria
When she performed for Queen Victoria.
And later, honouring her name,
King George the Fifth made her a Dame.

At her farewell, the Albert Hall
Gave many a cheer and curtain call.
She'd come a long way, after all,
This little girl from Montreal.

# SAMUEL STEELE
## (1849 - 1919)

*Samuel Steele was one of the first Mounties, and his long career took him west to police the Yukon during the Klondike Gold Rush, when he kept law and order in unruly places like Dawson City.*

Among the very first recruits
To don the Mounties' riding boots
And give the new force such appeal
Was Sergeant Major Samuel Steele.

His troop knew not what lay in store:
They trekked nine hundred miles and more
To keep their pledge and do their best
To police the new lands of the west.

They would establish law and order
Unlike the land across the border
Where guns and greed ruled every town
And soldiers hunted Indians down.
The Mounted Police wore coats of red
In case the natives turned and fled
Thinking they were that force of dread,
The U.S. Cavalry, instead.

For Sam Steele, life was never quiet:
He faced rebellion and riot,

Then in the 1890's came
The Gold Rush Years that made his name.

From way off down the Yukon River
Came rumours that made strong men quiver -
Rumours that would fulfill their dreams:
"It seems there's gold in them thar streams!"

So up towards the Passes then
Climbed thousands of gold-hungry men.
In struggling lines the great Stampede
Moved at a slow, laborious speed.

Many a man bore on his back
Possessions crammed into a pack.
Others dragged sleds, and quite a few
Used horses, dogs and reindeer too.
The leader of one Scottish group
Played bagpipes to inspire his troop.

There at the summit, Steele presided.
No man could pass, unless provided
With food and clothes and other gear
To last him for at least a year.
So, many times, those trudging men
Had to go down and back again
Until with their supplies at last
The Mounties would allow them past.

Frozen, and lashed by icy gales,

Many gave up the Gold Rush trails,
While others found they could not bear
The constant stench that hovered there
Of rotting horse-flesh, in the air.

Diseases claimed their victims too,
But twenty thousand made it through,
And down the Yukon with elation
They sailed towards their destination.

They found no end to their privation,
For Dawson City faced starvation.
Gold was in plentiful supply
But with no food, what could it buy?

The city struggled but survived -
And when snows melted, how it thrived!
Smart restaurants served caviar,
And liquor flowed in every bar.

The dance hall orchestras would play
As miners danced the night away.
While those whose tastes were more demure
Found that church choirs had more allure.

The Klondike Kings, the richest men,
Had fortunes spent, and made again.
Swiftwater Bill was one, so fine
He'd only take a bath in wine.
He paid, or so the story's told,

A Dance Hall girl her weight in gold.
One singer who was all the rage
Found golden nuggets thrown on stage.

The customers quite often paid
In gold dust which the barmen weighed.
These barmen who were deft and slick
Kept their hands damp, so some would stick.

For all the characters around
Apt nicknames could be always found:
Diamond-Tooth Gertie, Lime Juice Lil,
And Two-Step Louie, never still;
While Klondike Kate the dancing led,
A candelabra on her head.

This motley crowd Steele did police:
He made the rules and kept the peace,
Licensed the gambling clubs, objected
If Sunday wasn't well respected.

The Red Light District too obeyed
When told the girls could not parade
Till four p.m. had come and gone -
Then they were free to carry on.

Steele prosecuted as obscene
Comedians who mocked the Queen.
Con-men who did the miners down
He simply banished from the town.

But his attempts to stem corruption
Brought his career an interruption.
A devious, powerful politician
Dismissed him fast from his position.
Though many a protest and petition
From Dawson City's population
Pleaded for Sam Steele's restoration
The Klondike town would hear no more
The Lion of the Yukon's roar.

Though his career would have a score
Of other triumphs still in store,
It took the Yukon to reveal
The towering strength of Samuel Steele.

No wonder that the crowds turned out
To cry farewell, and cheer and shout,
And deemed it was a shameful pity
That Steele was leaving Dawson City.

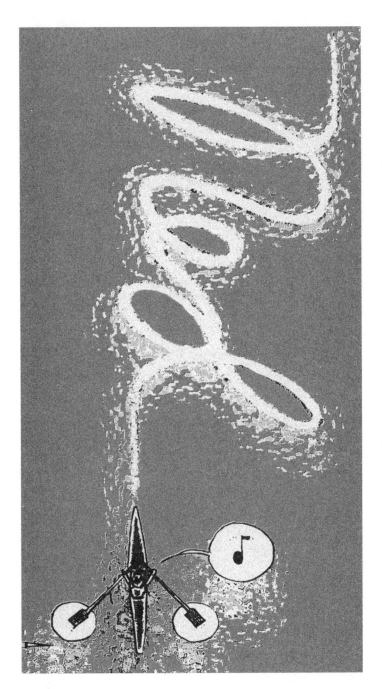

# NED HANLAN
## (1855-1908)

*Toronto-born Ned Hanlan spent much of his childhood in rowing boats, and became such a superb oarsman that in single sculls races he was five times world champion.*

Upon Toronto Island's shore
Ned Hanlan's father kept a store.
He told the boy, "It is the rule
For kids your age to go to school."
So Ned said, "Since I've got to go there,
The simplest way will be to row there."

For Ned loved rowing in his boat
And spent his boyhood years afloat.
By eighteen, he was doing well:
At single sculls he did excel
And was declared by those who know
The best in all Ontario.

He showed it was no idle claim:
Canadian Champion he became.
Soon after, south he took a trip
And won the U.S. Championship.

And then in England, on Thames' banks
Spectators thronged in peering ranks;

A hundred thousand cheered to see
Ned Hanlan row to victory.
At home, triumphant flags unfurled -
Ned was the Champion of the World!

And his successes then were stunning:
He won the title five years running.
With his moustache and curly hair
Ned was so smooth and debonair,
When he was racing anywhere
Excited crowds would always go
To watch their sporting hero row.
And as they cheered him long and loud,
Ned Hanlan entertained the crowd.
For such a speedy guy was Ned
That he was always way ahead;
So then he paused and smiled and gave
The watching crowds a friendly wave
And did some clowning while he'd stopped,
Pretending that his oars had dropped.

He'd row around in circles too
Until his rivals came in view;
Then as they panted up behind him,
Streaking ahead once more they'd find him.

In making light of his position
Ned followed in a great tradition:
New Brunswick fishermen did score
A big success some years before,

Becoming top World Champion Four.

They  used to carry wine to sup
Till their opponents caught them up,
And when they did, then just like Ned,
They'd promptly go full speed ahead.

Although today's Canadian crews
Don't carry with them crates of booze,
In triumph and in dedication
They look to Ned for inspiration.

# JAMES NAISMITH
## (1861-1939)

*James Naismith, from Almonte, Ontario, gained a doctorate in*
*theology in Montreal, He became a gymnastics teacher and*
*inspired his students by inventing the modern game of basketball.*

James Naismith studied at McGill:
Theology was his great skill.

But then, instead of being a preacher,
He worked as a gymnastics teacher.
And in that role, in Springfield, Mass.,
His greatest triumph came to pass.
There clever James amazed them all
When he invented basketball.

Lessons in his gymnasium
Had left his students feeling glum:
Some new game he must now devise
To make them want to exercise.

The janitor he then beseeches:
"Those baskets there, which carry peaches —
Please get me two of them, my friend,
And nail them up, at either end.
And when they're hanging on the wall
Then bring me, please, a soccer ball."

The janitor knew his propensity
For doing things with mad intensity —
And so he did what James requested
And soon this brand-new game was tested.

Although the students cried: "What fun!"
The score was only Nought to One.
They soon improved upon that figure,
And with each game the scores grew bigger.

This didn't please the janitor,
For after each and every score
The ball was trapped — he couldn't leave it,
But had to climb up and retrieve it.
He chuckled when the players fumbled,
But every time they scored, he grumbled.

He said: "Why was this game invented?
Those baskets have me quite demented.
I'm sorry now I ever got 'em:
Why don't I just cut off the bottom?"
He did, and Naismith with a whoop
Cried: "Great! Let's call the thing a hoop!"

The sport took off, and grew in fame —
But still it hadn't got a name.
The students said: "What we must do
Is call this new game after you. "

But James, being modest, thought it plain
That that would be a little vain.
It's just as well, for after all,
Who'd play a game called NAISMITHBALL?

# LOUIS CYR
## (1863 - 1912)

*French Canadian Louis Cyr defeated all challengers to be hailed*
*as the strongest man in the world, a title he would probably*
*still have if he were around today.*

Louis at birth the world astounds:
He weighs no less than eighteen pounds.
His father said, "I think we ought
To reinforce the baby's cot."

The beefy, blond and burly boy
Became his mother's pride and joy.
With curling tongs she curled his hair,
But no one dared to point or stare;
For Louis was, though groomed and curled,
The strongest man in all the world.

When just eighteen, he showed his force
By lifting up a full-grown horse.
One girl who watched him said, "I fear
I've lost my heart to Louis Cyr."
Melina Comtois was elated
To find her love reciprocated.

They married, but a former beau
Called David, loth to let her go,

Thought Louis' triumph he would check
By challenging him, in Quebec.

They chose a field all strewn with boulders
And tried to lift them on their shoulders.
They matched each other, rock by rock,
But one last boulder brought a shock.

Though David wrenched and strained to lift it
He found he simply couldn't shift it.
But Louis, as the cheers rang round,
Lifted that rock right off the ground.

Then later, Louis got the call
To join the police in Montreal.
When thugs attacked him in the street
He'd simply lift them off their feet.
Three men at once, on one occasion,
He carried thus into the station.

He toured in England where, amazed,
Crowds gasped to see the weights he raised.
Five hundred pounds he lifted there
With just one finger, in the air.
And quite as marvellous a feat
Was what the champion could eat.
He'd nonchalantly put away
Some twenty pounds of meat a day.

Back home, soon eighteen men he sat

Upon a plank - all very fat.
Without a groan, upon his back
He lifted up that paunchy pack.
They weighed four thousand pounds and more:
No strong man since has reached that score.

So let us honour, if you please,
This great Canadian Hercules.

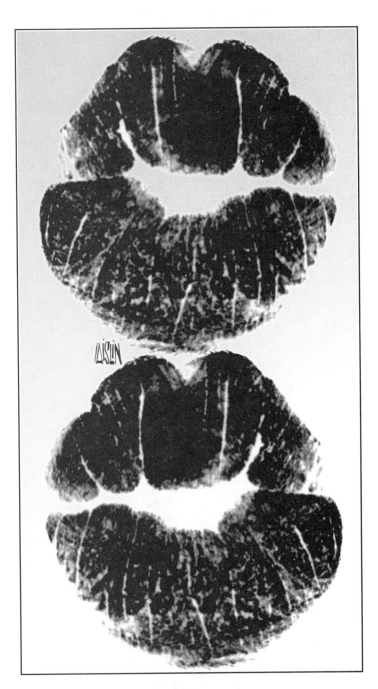

# MAY IRWIN
## (1863-1938)

*May Irwin was the stage name of May Campbell, who began her
theatre career in her teens and was soon an international star.
In the 1890's she caused a sensation when she featured in
the first kiss ever seen on the cinema screen.*

Mrs Campbell, best of mothers,
Like Mrs Worthington and others
Decided at a tender age
To put her daughters on the stage.

But Whitby in Ontario
Was not the place to make a show,
So Mrs Campbell thought she'd go
Across the lake to Buffalo.

The "Irwin Sisters" got the chance
To demonstrate their song and dance.
The show's producer was impressed -
Which proves that Mother knows what's best.
And soon the pair, so pert and pretty,
Became the toast of New York City.

Now even by the age of twenty
May Irwin had accomplished plenty.
She branched out in her stage career

And as an actress did appear.
Her theatre reputation grew
In London and in Paris too.

But stage success and foreign trips
Though glamorous, could not eclipse
The fame that came to her two lips.

For Thomas Edison, the man
With whom the movies first began,
Had got a plan that could not miss:
The filming of the first Screen Kiss.

In those first Motion Picture days
Short, flickering features were the craze
And trains filmed entering a station
Would cause an audience sensation.

Five days of filming were required,
Which made the kissers very tired
But got what Edison desired:
The cinemas were choc-a-bloc
As audiences gasped with shock
And moralists declared with gravity
The film would lead to gross depravity.

Just one more film was made by May
For she preferred the Great White Way,
And every time that she appeared
The audiences clapped and cheered.

She made  a fortune, with panache,
And with investments shrewd, not rash,
Survived unscathed the Wall Street crash.

May on the Thousand Islands made
A home where Glitterati stayed
And six grand pianos could be played.

At one of these, one idle day
Irving Berlin sat down to play
And with a flourish of his hand
Wrote Alexander's Ragtime Band.

May had produced, her fans to please,
Records, and books of recipes,
And in her sixties she could still
In any theatre, top the bill.

Flamboyant as the life she led,
May ordered that, when she was dead,
She should be buried, dressed in red.

# JACK MINER
## (1865-1944)

*Jack Miner was a hunter who turned conservationist.He established one of the very first bird sanctuaries, at Kingsville in Ontario, and pioneered the charting of bird migration patterns.*

No one has had ideals much finer
Than ornithologist Jack Miner.
Indeed it's true, in other words,
His work was strictly for the birds.

Yet wild life and its conservation
Were not at first his occupation.
In youth the game, each time he'd spot it,
He simply raised his gun and shot it.

In Kingsville as a teenage boy
His hunting skills he would employ.
Barefoot he'd go through wood and field
To see what kind of prey they'd yield.
A dead skunk was, he used to think,
At fifty cents well worth the stink.

Jack and his brother Ted could make
A fee for every rattlesnake.
When grouse became their chosen prey
They'd bring back twenty in a day.

They slaughtered deer and duck and moose
And learned to honk just like a goose.

When Ted was accidentally killed
Jack's heart with anguished grief was filled.
The consolation which he sought
Was found in church, and there he taught
With acclamation as a rule,
A boys' class in the Sunday School.
They found his stories most exciting
And they helped him  to master writing.

Quite soon he changed his attitude
To creatures he had once pursued.
He felt that they were more deserving
Of careful study and preserving.

He dug out ponds that geese would need
And planted trees and scattered seed,
Hoping the birds would understand
That here it would be safe to land.

The neighbours thought him somewhat weird,
Especially when no geese appeared.
It took four years till they'd begin
At last, to come and settle in.

Word must have spread, in Wild Goose Speak,
Passed eagerly from beak to beak,
That Kingsville was the place to seek.

And then it wasn't very long
Before each year the feathered throng
Was over fifty thousand strong.

His Sanctuary established, Jack
Thought their migration he would track.
He took a mallard and he put
A metal band around its foot;
Upon it his address was placed
So that the duck's flight could be traced.
Hundreds of miles south when it died,
Jack Miner soon was notified.

Thousands of birds each year were banded
So he'd discover where they landed.
Jack charted through this information
The wildfowls' pattern of migration.

Upon each band he also wrote
A short, uplifting Bible quote.
Who knows how many quick conversions
Resulted from those birds' excursions?

Jack toured and lectured and became
A famous conservation name.
Now Wildlife Week and his Foundation
Are part of his commemoration.
At Kingsville too the honking ranks
Of geese and ducks all voice their thanks!

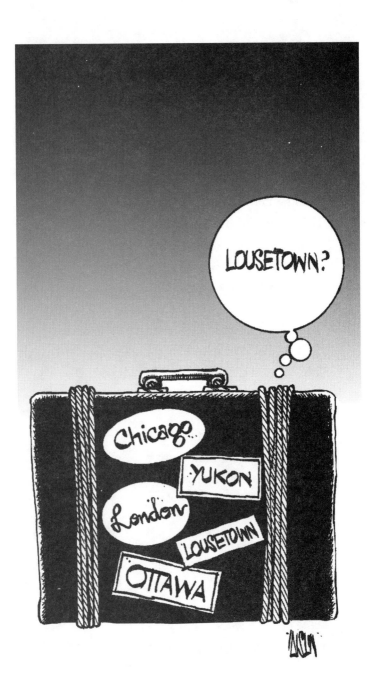

# MARTHA LOUISE BLACK
## (1866-1957)

*Martha Louise Black grew up in Chicago high society, but joined
the Klondike Gold Rush and went on to become 'Queen of the
Yukon' and only the second woman to sit in Canada's Parliament.*

Martha, since she was a girl,
Had loved Chicago's social whirl.
But in her thirties she set forth
To journey to the frozen north.

Her two sons with her parents stayed.
Her husband other plans had made:
He didn't want to stay around
And soon he was Hawaii-bound.
But his departure didn't grieve her
For Martha had the Gold Rush fever.

A boat to Skagway called Utopia
Led to a golden cornucopia -
Or so she hoped as, climbing higher
Dressed in Victorian attire
Consistent with her social class
She scaled the fearsome Chilkoot Pass.
Then through the rapids she must go
To Dawson City down below.

She staked some claims but didn't find

The riches that she had in mind.
So on the seamy side of town
In "Lousetown" Martha settled down.

Some very hard times there she knew -
Then found that she was pregnant too.
Her neighbours helped - at last with joy
They greeted Martha's baby boy.
Typhoid, a fire, a landslide fall -
Mother and child survived them all.

Chicago now had lost its lure -
The Yukon was her home for sure.
She loved its majesty - for hours
She roamed to seek its plants and flowers.
And having energy to spare
She started up a sawmill there.

She wed a lawyer called George Black.
Ambitious plans he did not lack,
And soon they came to fine fruition
When George attained a high position.
As Top Man he could take a bow:
Commissioner of the Yukon now.

A long way from the Town called Louse,
Now Martha moved to Government House,
And very soon there she was gaining
Great fame for lavish entertaining
As well as growing there to boot,
Her vegetables, flowers and fruit.

So celebrated had she grown,
As Lady Sourdough  she was known.
To those who liked a regal name,
Queen of the Yukon  she became.

When war came, George went off to France;
In London Martha took the chance
To publicize the Yukon there -
And she was honoured for her flair
In studying each flower variety
By the Royal Geographical Society.

Back home, George Black became M.P.
For Yukon's vast constituency.
When he was very ill, she said,
"I'll  campaign for the seat instead!"
Around the territory she trekked
Saying, "I'm the one you should elect."

And that's how Martha came to be
At seventy, a new M.P. -
The second woman who was sent
To Ottawa and Parliament.
There Martha joined Agnes Macphail,
The only two who were not male.

And after that career she planned
A book on her beloved land.
She buckled down and got it done -
And lived till she was ninety-one.

# STEPHEN LEACOCK
## (1869 – 1944)

*Stephen Leacock was one of the leading political economists of his time, and combined this profession with a satirical wit that made him a celebrated literary figure in Canada, the United States and Europe.*

Stephen Leacock got a thrill
From years of teaching at McGill.
He taught Political Economy
With really quite unusual bonhomie.
For, expert as he was in money,
He also was extremely funny.

Stephen was one of nature's wits
And had his audience in fits.
Today, as well as Economics,
He'd be among the stand-up comics.

His articles and stories too
Gave him a fame which grew and grew,
Till Stephen Leacock was the toast
Of countless fans from coast to coast.

So lots of money came his way,
And he himself was heard to say:
"My bread, upon the waters cast,
Came back to me as cake, at last!"

He is a type that's sorely missed —
A humorous economist.
Economists have got more numerous,
But would that one of them was humorous!

EMILY'S GROUP of 7

# EMILY CARR
## (1871-1945)

*Emily Carr, one of Canada's greatest and most original painters,*
*had to wait till she was fifty before her art got any wide recognition.*
*She grew up in Victoria, not the ideal setting for her eccentric and*
*volatile personality. But her great joy was travelling among the*
*distant forest and coastal communities of British Columbia, whose*
*lifestyle and totem pole art she recorded in her work.*

The Old World painters were inclined
To think that Art should be refined.
Canada's landscape they pooh-poohed:
"Those vistas are too vast and crude -
Unpaintable, that's what they are!"
But then, along came Emily Carr.

Her early sketches go right back
To charcoal portraits, on a sack.
Another childhood interest grew
In cherishing wild creatures too.
She tamed a squirrel and a crow -
And played guitar, and learned to sew.

In that strict family of nine
She was most often out of line,
And she remained throughout her life
A rebel who attracted strife.

Into the forest she would roam,
The local people's ancient home;
And so began her fascination
For many a centuries-old First Nation.

Some of the early friends she made
Lived near a Mission where she stayed.
Liking her warmth and sense of fun
They called her Klee Wyck  - 'Laughing One'.
(The Mission, treated with aversion
By contrast, made just one conversion.)

In England then she studied art;
A suitor who had lost his heart
Followed her there across the sea
And kept on asking, "Marry me!"

This happened several times a week,
And she'd refuse each time he'd speak.
In fact, though several suitors tried,
She never did become a bride.

Back home, Victoria's ways she mocked:
Her sisters were extremely shocked.
She smoked, her words were sometimes coarse -
She even rode astride  a horse!

Vancouver made a change of scene:
There, happier than she'd ever been,
She taught enthusiastically

Surrounded by her 'family' -
A dog, raccoons, a cockatoo,
Squirrels and chipmunks formed the crew.
Students, in spite of all these creatures,
Found Emily the best of teachers.

The places that she loved the most
Were in the woods and on the coast.
She got to know the vital roles
Played by the huge, carved totem poles.
She painted pictures of them, fearing
This art would soon be disappearing.

On Emily's journeys with her tent
A small menagerie always went.
The dog and cockatoo both came -
Even a vulture she'd made tame.

The villages and woods inspired her
And then a trip to Paris fired her:
She saw, instead of old precision,
A new art with a big, bold vision.
Now Emily with this art acquainted,
Knew how her  landscape could be painted.

But back at home, her striking style
Provoked a condescending smile.
They called the work of Emily Carr
Childish and clumsy and bizarre.
Her sister, blind to Emily's aims,

Told her, "I simply love  the frames!"

She kept on painting, loving best
The coast and forests of the West.
Their people's outlook she could share,
And found her firmest friendships there.

But even artists have to eat,
And Emily, to make ends meet,
Ran an apartment house, although
The dining-room made quite a show -
It doubled as a studio.
She felt this life was like a penance
And used to fight with all the tenants.

No fame or fanfares Emily knew
Till she was over fifty-two.
The National Gallery played a part:
It staged a show of West Coast Art.
At that exciting exhibition
Her art at last got recognition.

She'd been praised long ago in Paris:
Now she delighted Lawren Harris.
Soon she attained artistic heaven -
A show among the Group of Seven.
In Lawren Harris she had found
A mentor, fiery and profound.

He bought her paintings and declared:

"This Western genius must be shared.
If for a masterpiece you search,
Here's Emily's painting, Indian Church".

So Emily Carr at last became
In art a celebrated name;
And when she reached her seventieth year
Began a literary career.

Her stories brought her instant fame:
The first book's title was the same
As that fine nickname she had won -
Klee Wyck, which means The Laughing One.

TRANSLATION
"AND YOU'LL FIND MY HOME PAGE ON THE NET AT: www.guglielmomarconi.com..."

# GUGLIELMO MARCONI
## (1874 – 1937)

*Marconi pioneered the development of radio, and made many of his*
*key experiments in Canada.. He won the Nobel Prize in 1907.*

Marconi from his youth was tireless
In his experiments with wireless.
He thought he'd see his methods score
In messages from ship to shore.

His Government told poor Marconi
That all his schemes were pure boloney.
To England then Marconi came
And there began to make his name.
On lightships soon his gear was placed
And also used when yachts were raced.

Then Queen Victoria thought she might
Install it on the Isle of Wight.
She said: "My son the Prince of Wales
With riotous parties often sails.
Now I can learn, by dash and dot,
Just what he's up to, on his yacht."

And now Marconi had his eyes
Upon an even bigger prize.
He told investors: "I've a notion

To signal right across the ocean."
They knew that he was not a quitter,
And so they backed his new transmitter.

He built it very near Land's End
And got it all prepared to send,
But knew that no one would believe it
Until he'd somewhere to receive it.

In Newfoundland he built a station
To hear that first communication.
The aerial wire was quite a sight:
It was two hundred yards in height
And was suspended from a kite.

The first wire snapped — the second try
Rose up triumphant in the sky.
Marconi went indoors to hear,
And stuck the earphone in his ear.

He listened, worried, for a while,
Then gave a wide Italian smile.
He cried: "I hear it! Yes, yes, yes —
It's DOT-DOT-DOT — the letter S!
Wireless is here to stay, of course,
Thanks to myself, and Signor Morse.
The future beckons us: avanti!
We'll go and open the chianti!"

But cable companies with clout

Wanted to throw Marconi out.
Their plan, so grasping, vile and sinister,
Was foiled by Canada's Prime Minister.
Sir Wilfred Laurier said: "OK,
You may continue in Glace Bay,
And we shall put some funds your way."

So there on Nova Scotia's shore
More great successes lay in store.
The Governor-General released
The first transmission west to east.
Marconi then with joy was frantic,
For he had spanned the north Atlantic.
Soon many messages would fly
Thousands of miles across the sky.

And Canada he'd always thank
For seeing his intellectual rank,
When others thought him just a crank
And could not understand just what
Would come of that first DOT-DOT-DOT.

# LUCY MAUD MONTGOMERY
## (1874 – 1942)

*The author of the celebrated children's book,*
*"Anne of Green Gables", was born on Prince Edward Island,*
*where the book is set. She grew up there with her grandparents,*
*and only left when she married in 1911 and moved to Ontario,*
*where she continued to write more "Anne" stories.*

At four years old, in church one day,
Maud asked her aunt where Heaven lay.
She pointed upwards — Maud, ecstatic,
Assumed that it was in the attic.
In future, in whatever station,
She was less sure of its location.

She felt, when she was only nine,
That literature should be her line.
A blank verse poem she began;
Her father, not a tactful man,
Read it and said, as Maud's heart sank,
"You're right, my dear, it's very blank!"

Prince Edward Island was their home,
Although Maud's father liked to roam,
And several businesses did spawn
Way over in Saskatchewan.

His wife had died when Maud was two,

And so with grandparents she grew,
Upon a farm in Cavendish —
As fine a place as she could wish.
Its beauties, rural and inviting,
Were later to inspire her writing.

Grown up, she taught, and also wrote —
At 6 a.m., wrapped in a coat.
Her first paid work was to be seen
By readers of a magazine:
Verses for which her recompense
Was garden seeds, worth fifty cents.

A newspaper in Halifax
Gave her a job like any hack's:
Society columns, Tea-Time Chat,
Which she was very skilful at.
But all the time she was aspirin'
To be another Keats or Byron.

And then she wrote a novel which,
To her amazement, struck it rich.
Anne of Green Gables was the name
That launched her into wealth and fame.
It told how Anne the orphan came
To join the Cuthberts, at eleven,
And found Prince Edward Island heaven.

Anne's chattering ways, her wild elation,
Her passionate imagination,

Her eager schemes, her tough resilience,
Would bring her readers by the millions.

Though some reviewers made Maud sore —
(The New York Times called "Anne" a bore) —
The rest were most enthusiastic,
And Mark Twain thought the book fantastic.

Then a new life for Maud began,
With marriage to a clergyman.
She was a mother and a wife
And lived a calm, church-centred life.
Although she did it very well
She missed Prince Edward Island's spell,
And visits there would always be
A journey into memory.

Meanwhile, her readers all desired
More of the girl they so admired.
Anne of Green Gables was adored:
"Give us more stories!" they implored.

These Maud Montgomery supplied,
Though wearily she sometimes sighed:
"I wish that I could turn the tables,
And close the shutters on Green Gables!"

But still more fame would come her way:
There were two movies, and a play —
Yet Anne's creator got no pay.

Her contract, though she reached the heights,
Had never mentioned movie rights!

And now, though Maud herself is gone,
Her sparky heroine lives on,
And visitors from many lands
See where the house Green Gables stands.

And maybe, since she took the view
Reincarnation could be true,
Does Maud Montgomery see it too?

# ROBERT W. SERVICE
## – and those who came after him...
### (1874 – 1958)

*Robert Service's boisterous ballads about characters like Dangerous Dan McGrew earned him huge popularity as the Bard of the Yukon. He arrived from Scotland as a young man, and after years of roving he became a bank clerk in Whitehorse and Dawson City soon after the great Gold Rush days.*

The life of Robert W. Service
Would make most normal people nervous.
His journeys through the frozen wastes
Were not to everybody's tastes —
But though in life they'd do without them,
They simply loved to read about them,
And with his books he was, henceforth,
The Bard of the Canadian North.

Brought up in Scotland, as a lad
A taste for verse he always had,
And on his poetry he'd work,
When in the bank he was a clerk.
When done with debtors and with creditors,
He'd send his poems off to editors,
Who published his poetic flights
In People's Friend and Scottish Nights.

Then of the banking life he tired:

By wanderlust he was inspired.
Young Robert said he couldn't wait
To board a ship and emigrate.
With joy he stood upon the deck
To watch the docking at Quebec.
He had a ticket to the west
And just five dollars in his vest.

The crowded train moved down the track —
He slept upon the luggage rack;
And on that journey he was quite
A striking, if a curious, sight.
For he was dressed like Buffalo Bill:
His feet high circus-boots did fill,
And on his head, so debonair-o,
He wore a dashing black sombrero.

Fine, if in movies he'd appeared —
In Winnipeg he just looked weird.

But as the train went on and on
Most of his gear was quickly gone.
He had to sell things, one by one:
His suit, his camera, his gun.

Yet on the Rockies as he gazed
He felt ecstatic and amazed.
To a Pacific dawn he woke
Elated, eloquent, and broke.

And so his wandering life began:
He was a farm hand, dairyman,
An orange picker, lumberjack,
Dug tunnels for a trolley track,
Became a hobo and a bum,
Slept on the ground, his cold limbs numb;
At farm doors tried to cadge a meal,
And even chewed banana peel.

In bunks he felt the bed bugs bite,
And in his notebooks tried to write.
His mates found this a bit dismaying,
But they enjoyed his banjo playing.

He finally rejoined the ranks
Of humble clerks who toil in banks;
And soon they said, to Robert's joy:
"You're going to the Yukon, boy!"

By boat to Skagway, then by rail,
He followed that old Gold Rush Trail.
In Whitehorse for three years he stayed —
The brightest move he ever made.

For there, the gateway to the North,
Sourdoughs to him their tales poured forth
Of Gold Rush Times, of bar-room fights,
Of gaudy, bawdy days and nights,
Of booze and broads, ferocious feuds,
Grafters and gamblers and dudes,

Of gold dust gleaming in the pan
And Mounties, out to get their man,
Of strange things done in the midnight sun
—And Robert noted every one.

He noted too, with style and grace,
The wild, white beauty of the place.
He'd walk on snowshoes through the night,
The far, cold moon his only light;
And as he walked with quiet tread
The verses came into his head.

Soon Dan McGrew had been created
And frozen Sam McGee cremated;
But in a cupboard, put away,
They didn't see the light of day.
At last he thought: "This makes no sense —
I'll publish, at my own expense."

The publisher sent back his money;
"Your verse," he said, "is fine and funny!"
So out that first slim volume came:
Songs of a Sourdough was its name.
It brought its author instant fame —
And fortune, for the writing game
Earned more than many a Gold Rush claim.

But Robert was a thrifty feller —
He kept his bank job as a teller.
To Dawson City he transferred;

The Klondike too his name had heard.
His new mates, bowing to his skill,
Cried: "Here's the Bard of Bawdyville!"

And in the mess, that bunch of boys
Would whoop it up with so much noise
That Robert then could only write
Well after midnight every night.

He left the bank and closed his till,
But, keen to stay in Dawson still,
He found a cabin on a hill.
There, walking he would often go
At seventy-two degrees below,
With icicles upon his breath
And danger of a frostbite death.

There, washing sometimes wasn't nice,
Rubbing down with chunks of ice.
Yet Robert Service thought it great,
And wrote The Trail of '98.

For many years he wrote his tales,
Long after he had left those trails.
And in those Klondike tales he told,
He truly struck a vein of gold.

Those characters delight us still:
There's Chewed-Ear Jenkins, Barb-Wire Bill,
And all that brash and boisterous crew:

The Ragtime Kid, and Dan McGrew,
And Sam McGee who warmed right through,
And, of course, the Lady known as Lou.

Though long before these fine creations,
The living culture of First Nations
Had viewed this land with subtle eyes
And shaped their arts to match its size,
Woven webs of songs and stories
Harmonized with all its glories.

Service was first to use with pride
The English language, versified,
To conjure up with joy and zest
The wild ways of his new-found West.

Since then, Canadians present
A literary firmament,
Where John McRae his talent wields
While poppies grow in Flanders Fields,
And Leacock, the economist,
Becomes a famous humorist.

Before him, Haliburton came:
His Clockmaker, Sam Slick by name,
Gained international acclaim.
While Pauline Johnson got together
Her poetry, in Flint and Feather,
And Lucy Maud Montgomery's Anne
Her sparkling careeer began.

Later, novelists arose
Whose names now everybody knows.
Robertson Davies earned high praise
With essays, stories, books and plays,
And the tales of Margaret Laurence
Brought her praise in mighty torrents.

Mordecai Richler, most provoking,
Makes people ask how much he's joking.
And lively too was the arrival
Of Margaret Atwood's book, Survival.
Her verse and novels are a hit
In all Canadian English Lit.
When she describes the bush, we find
She also maps the human mind.

Alice Munro touches our hearts
With all her storyteller's arts.
Michael Ondaatje never shirks
Delving where myth or marvel lurks,
And Farley Mowat's loved, it's clear,
Not just by People of the Deer.

For Carol Shields, no honour fits her
Better than prizes like Pulitzer:
That's where her fine Stone Diaries took her —
And it was listed for the Booker!

The reading public too are certain
To hail the works of Pierre Berton.
To The Last Spike he never fails
To keep the show upon the rails.

The list of works and those who write 'em
Goes on and on, ad infinitum,
Too rich and vast to classify
(Unless of course you're Northrop Frye) —
Which shows the future's safe and sure
For good Canadian literature,
So full of power and wit and radiance —
Here's to all literary Canadians!

# LORD BEAVERBROOK
## (1879-1964)

*Lord Beaverbrook was born Max Aitken and grew up in New
Brunswick. He showed an early talent for making money especially
by company mergers, and when he went to England he used his
wealth to become a newspaper tycoon, and his personality to make
his mark among the top politicians of his time.*

Max Aitken's earliest experience
Was spent among the Presbyterians;
But though his father was a preacher
Morals weren't Max's greatest feature.
His raffish youth, though, did reveal
His tendency to wheel and deal.

By eighteen, he'd been seen to dally
With frozen meats, a bowling alley,
The law and the insurance trade -
And then the mergers game he played.

Small companies gave Max the urge
To buy them up and then to merge,
And by these slick amalgamations
To fashion giant corporations.

In property, cement and steel,
Max took the plunge and did the deal.
He sidestepped any legal hitches

And made himself enormous riches.

So off to England then he went
And soon got into Parliament.
Fellow-Canadian Bonar Law
Max Aitken's great potential saw
And helped his progress, for he knew
That he  was from New Brunswick too.

  Max got political rewards:
A peerage in the House of Lords.
He wondered then what name would seem
To suit him, and recalled a stream
Where as a child he used to look
At beavers swimming - so he took
The name of Baron Beaverbrook.

As well as being a Lord he soon
Became a newspaper tycoon.
He craved the power and the success
He thought would come with the Express.

He was a brash, hands-on proprietor -
His staff all wished that he was quieter,
But they endured the barking tone
That roared instructions down the phone.

Luxuriously the Beaver  sat
In country house or London flat,
French villa, or on faraway

Verandahs in Montego Bay,
And like some medieval Czar
Controlled his lackeys from afar.

At Max's orders they'd crusade
For policies like Empire Trade.
While Hitler's threats grew more and more
And Europe knew what lay in store
Lord Beaverbrook's three papers bore
The headline, THERE WILL BE NO WAR!

When war came, Beaverbrook would get
A place in Churchill's Cabinet -
For Churchill was just one great name
Whose friendship Beaverbrook could claim.
His magnetism would delight
The politicians, left and right:
Nye Bevan, Michael Foot, Lloyd George -
Strong bonds with all of them he'd forge.

At dinner in his country house
The great and famous would carouse;
But first for cocktails, Max would fix
The daiquiris he loved to mix.

In politics, his guests all knew
He was a powerful fixer too -
And how he loved to stir the brew!
His wealth and contacts gave the means
To wheel and deal behind the scenes,

And secretly he'd interfere
With many a promising career.

In machinations and intrigues
Old Max was in the Major Leagues.
No wonder that, while many fêted him
A lot of others really hated him.

By Churchill's wife he was abused:
"A microbe!" was the term she used.
He had vendettas, tried to flatten
The reputation of Mountbatten,
Detested Baldwin, growled and glowered
If someone mentioned Noel Coward.

Yet all the schemes he liked to cherish
Were mostly doomed to fail and perish.
He'd tell his papers: "Rant and rage,
And put my views on every page!
The public then will quickly gauge
Just what the only way to vote is."
The public simply took no notice!

One of his editorial crew
Remarked when he was feeling blue:
"In Fleet Street, one great fact is true -
Experience to me has taught it:
No cause is lost, till we  support it!"

Lord Beaverbrook, forever proud

Of his home province, there endowed
Town halls and squares and rinks for skaters,
Organs and steeples and theaters.
There, almost everywhere you look
You find the name of Beaverbrook.

As H.G.Wells was wont to say:
"Perhaps his soul's alive today
Making, before the final knell,
A merger between Heaven and Hell!"

# MACK SENNETT
## (1880 – 1960)

*Mack Sennett, the pioneer of silent film comedy and creator of the*
*Keystone Cops, was born and grew up in Quebec. After stage work*
*as a chorus boy and vaudeville artist, he went into movies, and*
*began his celebrated career as actor and director.*

"My name," said actor Michael Sinnott,
"Has really got no glamour in it."
Did it have more, one wonders, when it
Was altered to become MACK SENNETT?

Born in Quebec when times were tough,
He knocked around, lived fast and rough,
And then decided that the thing
He'd really like to do was sing.

But he got little fame or joy
Performing as a chorus boy,
Though he acquired some comic skill
In burlesque shows and vaudeville.

At movies then he had a go;
Producers didn't shout: "Bravo!"
And snubbed him with: "We'll let you know."
Sennett was not discouraged, though,
And still hung round the studio.

Eventually he got a role
In Griffith's film, The Curtain Pole.
The curtain rose on his career,
And Sennett's screen success was clear.

Soon he was one of Griffith's troupe,
With Mary Pickford in the group.
D. W. Griffith would select
Mack Sennett also to direct.

And then he made a great advance:
Two bookmakers took quite a chance,
Deciding they'd provide finance.
And that was the inauguration
Of Keystone Pictures Corporation.

Soon Sennett's comedies were tops,
Especially the Keystone Cops.
The audiences clapped and cheered
When that fantastic Force appeared.

By crafty crooks those Cops were goaded,
Trains ran them down, and cars exploded.
In wild pursuits and hectic chases
The custard pies festooned their faces.
Those flickering reels of celluloid
Had audiences overjoyed.

While policemen did their slapstick duties,

Mack also filmed his Bathing Beauties,
A line of girls with twinkling eyes
And costumes draping wiggling thighs.
Though, seeing today how stars divest,
Mack Sennett's belles look overdressed.

Of all the Beauties in Mack's stable
His best and greatest love was Mabel.
Sennett, for all his comic antics,
Was truly one of life's romantics,
And Mabel Normand was by far,
In films and life, his brightest star.

So many great careers would grow
From Sennett's Keystone Studio.
The young Charles Chaplin started there;
He spotted, too, Frank Capra's flair.

There Gloria Swanson got her chance,
And Harry Langdon he'd advance.
Bing Crosby starred there for a spell,
And Fatty Arbuckle as well.
Though once they all were up and started
To other studios they departed.

When talkies came, so cheered and fêted,
Mack Sennett's style looked rather dated.
His comedies seemed far less funny,
And soon poor Mack lost all his money.

He said farewell to Hollywood,
But couldn't part from it for good.
Though some might think him on the shelf,
In several films he played himself.

When honoured by the Film Academy,
He said: "Well, they can't think so bad o' me!"
And Hollywood Cavalcade would be
Mack Sennett's film biography.

A stage show honours him as well:
His tale's a splendid one to tell,
For he had played a major part
In shaping cinematic art.

The boy who started in Quebec
To Hollywood had made the trek,
And in that silent era he
Became the King of Comedy.

His Keystone Cops remain immortal
Wherever audiences chortle
At custard pies and slapstick farces,
And policemen falling on their arses.

# ELIZABETH ARDEN
## (1882-1966)

*Elizabeth Arden was born Florence Nightingale Graham, in
Ontario. Believing that 'women have the right to be beautiful',
she set about helping them with treatments and cosmetics that
brought her world-wide fame and fortune.*

This fact not many people know:
Elizabeth Arden's name was Flo.
Woodbridge Ontario was the site
Where little Flo first saw the light.
The Grahams' baby didn't wail
When christened Florence Nightingale,
But that was quite a mouthful, so
She quickly shortened it to Flo.

She did try nursing, but was sure
Rather than medicines to cure
She would prefer to make and sell
Products to beautify the well.

So to the kitchen then she went
Determined to experiment.
The stench resulting from her labours
Asphyxiated all the neighbours.

But Flo, in spite of their vexation,

WHAT ELIZABETH ARDEN USED...

WHAT ELIZABETH ARDEN NEEDED...

Knew she had found her true vocation,
And though her father went berserk,
Off to New York she went to work.

And there a new career begins:
Tight straps pull in the clients' chins
While expert hands massage the faces
And cream smooths out Time's tell-tale traces.
This, Beauty Parlours tell their clients,
Is not just pampering, but Science.

Ladies once thought it would deprave you
Improving on what Nature gave you,
But what once smacked of impropriety
Was now the rage in High Society.

Soon Flo fulfilled her bold intent
To start her own establishment.
She teamed up with Elizabeth Hubbard
Who'd many potions in her cupboard,
And with Flo's skills and selling flair
They seemed to be the perfect pair.

But Flo's hot temper led to strife
Which happened often in her life.
Flo on her own then staked her claim
But kept Elizabeth's first name.
The Arden which she added on
Came from a work by Tennyson.

Her salon in Fifth Avenue
Into a massive empire grew.
At first when times were rather lean
She got there first, to sweep and clean.
The salon, though, was made luxurious
And there she reigned, petite and furious.
She sacked employees by the score;
 One girl said, "Working there is more
Like being in a revolving door."

But before long demand was huge
For Arden face powders and rouge,
Mascaras, cleansing creams, and oceans
Of tonics, muscle oils and lotions,
All claiming that they'd bring perfection
To every customer's complexion.

Elizabeth had tried herself
Each product that was on the shelf.
She practiced, such was her persistence,
Many times too on her assistants.

As well as a persuasive title
She knew that packaging was vital
And used her fine designing skills
On ribbons, furbelows and frills.

In spite of its refined appeal
The Beauty Game was not genteel:
Elizabeth had nerves of steel

And battled all along the line
With her great rival, Rubenstein.

They never met and never spoke,
Treating each other as a joke.
The rival's name was never said:
"That woman" was the term instead.

She took up yoga and devised
A room where clients exercised,
And made, with outcome most rewarding,
The world's first exercise recording.

And then in Maine, for something new,
She pioneered the Health Spa too.
Among the treatments she would deem
Essential to the day's regime
Were headstands, Youth Masks for the skin
And also baths in paraffin.

Soon as a hobby she was able
To buy herself a racehorse stable.
She painted it pink, white and blue,
And even had piped music too.
In baby-talk she'd bill and coo
To stop her "darlings" feeling blue.

Though jockeys chuckled at her notions
They rubbed the horses with her lotion.
Thanks maybe to these airs and graces

Her horses won a lot of races.

She married twice, had two divorces,
But stayed devoted to her horses.
At eighty, still alert and keen
She ruled her empire like a queen.

Thousands whom she'd beautified
Turned out to mourn her when she died.
One woman found the strange thought strike her:
"Miss Arden dead?  That's so unlike her!"

# LOUIS B. MAYER
## (1885 – 1957)

*As a child, Louis B.Mayer came with his family to settle in
Saint John, New Brunswick, where he grew up and worked in his
father's scrap metal business. He moved to New England and
prospered as a film distributor, then as a producer. He went on to
found the MGM Studios and become one of the most powerful,
feared and revered figures in Hollywood.*

To New Brunswick – the port of Saint John –
Louis' people from Russia had gone.
Though scrap metal dealing
Was not too appealing
What deals he would do later on!

With film distribution he scored,
Then with Metro and Goldwyn on board,
He teamed up with them
To found M.G.M.
And the Lion in the cinemas roared!

He was Hollywood mogul and czar –
Film careers he could make or could mar.
Both Garbo and Gable
Were in Louis' stable
So were Hepburn, and Hedy Lamarr.

He changed writers' work without pity;

His retort when they raged could be witty:
"The Bible we call
The best book of all –
And who wrote that book? A Committee!"

His studio for years Mayer led;
At his funeral, enemies said
That of hundreds who came
Quite a few had one aim:
To make very sure he was dead!

# GREY OWL
## (1888 – 1938)

*Archibald Belaney grew up in the south of England, but went to
Canada and adopted a false Indian identity as Grey Owl.
He worked as a trapper and then became a conservationist, keeping
his invented disguise throughout the lecture tours which made him
a spectacular success in Canada, the USA and England.*

Believing in your own publicity
Is quite a common eccentricity,
And Grey Owl fostered the belief
That he was practically a Chief.

He dyed his hair the deepest black
And with a hide thong tied it back.
He tried to walk the Indian way
And learned to speak in Ojibway.

He made sure nobody recalled
That his real name was Archibald,
Pretending that it wasn't true
That he was English through and through.

Brought up in Hastings as a child,
His ways were always somewhat wild.
He'd whoop and hoot, alarm the teachers
With snakes and mice and other creatures.
"I'll train for life outdoors," said he –

And slept all night up in a tree.

At eighteen, following his bent,
Away to Canada he went.
He learned to trap and to canoe,
And Indian skills and stories too.

And so began, bizarre and zany,
The life of Archibald Belaney.
In this most colourful of lives
He wooed and married several wives –
Not always bothering, what is more,
Divorcing from the wife before.

The one who gave him greatest joy
He met among the Iroquois.
Anahareo was her name;
She really shaped what he became.
She thought wild animals deserved
To be protected and preserved.

For conservation Archie opted –
Two baby beavers they adopted,
And soon a colony was planned.
The Parks Department thought it grand
And made a film whose stars so furry
Made audiences' eyes go blurry:
So cute and playful and endearing,
The Beaver Family had them cheering.

And soon with books and lectures too
Grey Owl's renown just grew and grew.
Through Canada, the USA
And England too he made his way
And there in London he was seen
Performing for the King and Queen.

As each rapt audience applauded
They didn't know they'd been defrauded,
And this fine Brave, so strong and wise,
Was simply Archie, in disguise.

But though he wasn't what he seemed
It was a worthy dream he dreamed:
A peaceful world where Man would be
To Nature, friend – not enemy.

At only fifty, Grey Owl died.
His hoaxes then he could not hide,
And those who'd praised him to the skies
Now scorned his masquerading lies.
So Grey Owl's pose as man of mystery
Was very soon consigned to history.

But now – the final accolade –
A Grey Owl movie has been made.
Pierce Brosnan, resting from James Bond,
The mantle of Grey Owl has donned –
Which must, wherever he may be,
Have Archie giving hoots of glee!

# AGNES MACPHAIL
## (1890-1954)

*In 1921 Agnes Macphail became the first woman MP elected
to Canada's House of Commons. She braved derision and hostility
to champion the causes she believed in.*

Women voted since 1918
But no woman MP there had been
    Until Agnes Macphail
    Startled many a male
By invading the Ottawa scene.

She scorned male cabals and Old Pallery
And was mocked by the Press in the gallery.
    They all thought her bats,
    For she wouldn't wear hats
And suggested MPs cut their salary!

She withstood all the glares and the jeers
And stayed there for near twenty years.
    She campaigned for Disarmers
    And miners and farmers,
Till at last all the jeers turned to cheers.

# AIMEE SEMPLE McPHERSON
# (1891 – 1944)

*Aimee Semple McPherson – the two surnames came from her
first two husbands – grew up near Ingersoll, Ontario, and soon
discovered an oratorical flair that would make her name
and fortune as a barnstorming evangelist across North America
and in Europe and Australia too.*

The young Aimee Semple McPherson
Publicity-wise, was no dunce:
She grew famous, performing in person,
Some great evangelical stunts.

She would go to a crossroads and proudly
Proclaim that her work was the Lord's;
She would stand on a chair and pray loudly,
And the people came flocking in hordes.

Soon Aimee was driving them frantic,
Such a barnstorming style she could boast.
She wowed them beside the Atlantic
And across to the far western coast.

With marvellous Minnie, her mother,
To manage all matters financial,
One triumph led on to another
And her fortune grew very substantial.

Such worldly wealth pleased Aimee Semple
As she fervently preached the Good News:
She founded her very own Temple
Where five thousand could sit in the pews.

One day, Aimee suddenly vanished
From a beach not too far from her Church.
Thoughts of stunts then could hardly be ban-
ished,
Though thousands came flocking to search.

In a month she turned up, full of fury,
Crying: "Kidnappers captured me, folks!"
But lawyers before a Grand Jury
Accused her of staging a hoax.

The courts in the end didn't charge her
Though many still thought it a plot,
But her church congregation grew larger
And so did the money she got!

Her family relations grew bitter,
With many a law-suit and feud.
Her mother then claimed Aimee hit her,
And got lots of cash when she sued.

But Aimee's support just got stronger
And she stayed at the top of the tree –
And we wonder, if she had lived longer,
What a hit she'd have made, on TV".

# MARY PICKFORD
## (1893 – 1979)

*Mary Pickford was a flourishing child actress on the Canadian
stage until she went first to Broadway and then into movies,
becoming one of the most idolized stars of the silent screen.*

Born in Toronto, Gladys Smith
Became a cinematic myth.
The glamorous Gladys rose to fame
With Mary Pickford as her name.

When she was three, her father died.
"How shall we live?" her mother sighed.
And then at five, on theatre stages,
Young Gladys started earning wages.

The child star flourished — at fourteen
She entered on the Broadway scene.
Though in some films she'd take a part,
She felt that it demeaned her art.

D. W. Griffith was the man
With whom her film career began.
He was a most perceptive fella:
He picked her out for Cinderella.

Such waif-like roles there were aplenty:

Poor Little Rich Girl, Sweet and Twenty,
Oh, Uncle! and The Little Teacher —
In countless films did Mary feature.

In all her winsome, child-like parts
She broke the audiences' hearts.
And very soon, with growing fame,
The national Sweeheart she became.

But though her roles were coy and cute,
Her business sense was most astute.
She and her mother, it would seem,
Made up a great financial team.
Their entry to negotiations
Gave movie moguls palpitations.

From forty dollars every week,
Much higher earnings she would seek.
In just two years they sure got bigger:
Ten thousand weekly was the figure!

She was among the first to see
A star could ask a massive fee
And make the Studios agree.

The moguls couldn't win the fight:
It took, to get her contract right,
According to Sam Goldwyn's stricture,
Much longer than to make the picture!

In 1919, stars she knew —
Fairbanks and Chaplin, Griffith too —
With Mary thought they'd have a go
At forming their own Studio.

United Artists had appeared:
The movie moguls scoffed and sneered.
"The lunatics" — as one did style 'em —
"Have taken over the asylum!"

Mary and Douglas Fairbanks wed,
And many gossip columns fed.
In lavish style they cut a dash
And made, and spent, a lot of cash.

A rambling mansion was the scene
Where they both reigned like King and Queen.
Pickford and Fairbanks thought they'd let it
Be called the name of PICKFAIR — get it?!

And still the audiences raved
For Mary in the roles they craved:
So impish, innocent, demure —
A Pollyanna, sweet and pure.
Mary was typecast, to her rage,
And frozen at that girlish age.

She said: "I'll show they've had their day,
These simpering maidens I portray —
I'll get my ringlets cut away!"

She did — and if you want to see 'em,
They're in a Hollywood museum.

Mary Pickford still survived
When talking pictures first arrived.
An early Oscar she would get
To praise her acting in Coquette.

Mary was nearly forty now,
And soon she made her final bow.
A Western was the last we'd see
Of her, in 1933.

At Grauman's Theater, where stars went
To put their prints in the cement,
Smaller than any, Mary's pair
Of tiny hands are frozen there:
Memorials to Gladys Smith,
Canadian cinematic myth.

# BILLY BISHOP
## (1894 – 1956)

*Born in Owen Sound, Ontario, Billy Bishop was an*
*unruly student who came into his own as an ace fighter pilot*
*during the First World War. He shot down a record 72 enemy*
*planes and won many medals, including the Victoria Cross.*
*His courage and his flamboyant personality made him a popular*
*celebrity, and he lived to play an important role with the*
*Royal Canadian Air Force in World War Two.*

No great delight young Billy found
In life at school in Owen Sound;
Nor did he seem to get much knowledge
At Kingston's Military College.

By discipline he was repelled –
In fact, he nearly got expelled.
But Billy said: "Before you bar me,
I'm going off to join the army!"

He went to England then to train.
Drilling one day, in mud and rain,
He saw above, a fighter plane.
High up it flew, alone and free;
Billy decided: "That's for me!
This army life is such a chore:
I'll join the Royal Flying Corps."

Many Canadians shared his aim:
As pilots, twenty thousand came.

Now Billy, zooming through the air,
Was brave and brash and debonair.
Down through the clouds his plane would
swoop
Then nonchalantly loop the loop.
He chased his quarries with ferocity
Pursuing them at high velocity;
He'd dart and dive, machine-guns blazing –
His accuracy was amazing.

His style was just a bit ham-handed –
He damaged aircraft when he landed.
One general was a bit dismayed
When Billy, undercarriage splayed,
Crashed right in front of his parade.

One colleague said: "Though Billy's got
Great talent as a brilliant shot
An expert pilot he is not!"

But though he was inclined to crash
He had such daring and panache
His score of planes shot down was higher
Than any other Air Force flyer.
He once shot five down in one day –
And many medals came his way.

And somehow Billy did contrive
Through years of war, to stay alive.
Home as a hero then he came
To celebrations, cheers and fame.

The war was won, but Billy still
Craved the excitement and the thrill.
A company he put in place
With Billy Barker, fellow ace.

They said: "What Torontonians need
To start their weekends off with speed
Are aircraft fitted with pontoons
To land on lakes among the loons.
We'll save them hours and hours of driving
And soon our service will be thriving!"

But then they squandered any gains
By buying two old fighter planes
To use their flying skills at once
At fairs and shows, by doing stunts.

Sadly, the first big show to hire them
Immediately had to fire them:
The pilots, feeling blithely manic,
Dived at the grandstand, causing panic.

Then, though the thrills and spills were less,
In business sales, he had success.
In World War Two, his reputation

Enthused the Air Force of the nation.

His fame and talent were well suited
To get Canadians recruited,
And Billy Bishop would be partial
To recognition as Air Marshal.
No fitter honour could be found
To praise the boy from Owen Sound.

# WINNIE THE POOH

*The origins of A.A.Milne's famous character can be traced back to a*
*Canadian bear cub which became a First World War army mascot.*

The Second Infantry Brigade
By train a wartime journey made:
White River in Ontario
Was on the route they had to go,
And Captain Colebourn spotted there
A most enchanting baby bear.

The Captain promptly thought he'd get
The little black cub as a pet.
He said, "I'll mark my home town's fame
By making Winnipeg its name."

Soon known as Winnie, she was made
The mascot of the whole brigade.
In England where they went to train
They had a camp on Salisbury Plain.
Winnie was petted, praised and fed,
And slept beneath the Captain's bed.

But when the troops went off to war
Winnie could stay with him no more.
The Zoo was asked, for the duration,
To give the bear accommodation.

Soon, capering around her cage
Winnie the bear was all the rage.
She'd roll around and wave her paws
And revel in the crowd's applause.

The Captain, when the war had ended,
Thought Winnie's winning ways were splendid.
It would be best for her, he knew,
To leave her there in London Zoo.

The children loved her - there was one
Called Christopher, A.A.Milne's young son,
Who at the age of five or six
Was just delighted with her tricks.

His father wrote, to please the boy,
A tale that children would enjoy
In which a teddy bear did feature;
Winnie was what he called the creature,
After the bear in London Zoo
And so was born Winnie the Pooh.

The real bear died in quiet old age -
Her namesake though still holds the stage,
Alive and kicking on the page.

White River in commemoration
Now holds an annual celebration
To honour Captain Colebourn's name
And that young cub who rose to fame:
Winnie, the bear who gained such glory
By starring in a children's story.

WHAT HAS BEEN CANADA'S MOST IMPORTANT
EXPORT TO BRITAIN?

☐ Newsprint?
☐ Toilet Paper?
☐ Roy Thomson?

# ROY THOMSON
## (1894 – 1976)

*Starting work at fourteen as a coal-yard clerk in Toronto, Roy
Thomson became a radio salesman and then went on to control a
world-wide media empire with hundreds of newspapers,
magazines and radio and television stations. He also achieved his
two most cherished ambitions: to be the propietor of the London
Times, and a member of the House of Lords.*

There was a barber's son called Roy
Who roamed Toronto's streets
And from his teens, his greatest joy
Was reading balance sheets.

He worked at selling radios
With flair and dedication
Till finally the chance arose
To buy a radio station.

Soon other stations came his way
And so did several papers.
More chances turned up every day
For Roy's commercial capers.

With love of wheeler-dealing
He was well and truly smitten;
Now he said: "I'll set them reeling
Way over there in Britain."

The Brits at first resented
This Canadian invasion
But the money he presented
Was a wonderful persuasion.

He soon became a social swell
With power and position
And even back at home as well
He got some recognition.

Toronto's Scottish Regiment
Said: "Be our Colonel." – "Yes!"
Cried Roy, "and my intent's
To wear full Scottish dress!"

One Scots employee made the crack:
"He has me near to tears –
As for the kilt, he's set it back
At least a hundred years!"

Roy said: "I never try to tame
My editorial pressmen."
Then Beaverbrook said: "I'm the same –
But then, I just hire Yes-Men!"

Oh, how Roy envied Beaverbrook!
And how he would determine
To be, like him, by hook or crook,
A Lord, with robes and ermine!

Not all Canadians would greet
With joy, Roy's royal rewards,
The day Lord Thomson took his seat
In Britain's House of Lords.

But now that Roy had scaled the heights
He longed for higher climbs:
Voraciously he set his sights
Upon the London Times.

The powers-that-be might fulminate
As Thomson schemed and stalked;
His Lordship only had to wait:
He knew that money talked.

They watched this brash Canadian guy
Do what he felt he must:
Grab major slices of the pie
And join the Upper Crust!

A third Canadian tycoon
Has said: "Now look at me –
I too will be a Lord quite soon,
And that will make it three!"

But Monsieur Chrétien saw his scheme –
"I veto it," said Jean.
"Let Conrad of his peerage dream –
The answer it is Non!"

"I'll sell my papers!" Conrad swore,
"You've barred my just rewards,
And now I'll never take the floor
In Britain's House of Lords."

So Conrad Black has been upstaged,
To Jean he had to bow.
But Roy himself would be enraged
To see what's happened now.

Today, he'd have to do without
Big Ben's melodious chimes –
Most of the Lords are booted out
And Murdoch owns The Times!

# BEATRICE LILLIE
## (1898-1989)

*Beatrice Lillie began her performing career as a member of the Lillie Trio with her mother and sister in Toronto. She went on to become a comedienne who delighted audiences on both sides of the Atlantic, as well as such stars as Charlie Chaplin and Noel Coward.*


Bea said: "At twelve, I just stopped growing -
My nose, however, kept on going."
Although she felt her nose lacked charm
It sure did her career no harm.

Her marvelously mobile face
Could make them laugh with one grimace.
From slapstick falls to caustic wit
Her style made Bea a world-wide hit.
They called her, with those beads she twirled,
The funniest woman in the world.

But as a girl, a taste she had
For ballads serious and sad.
The one she really used to love
Was Oh, for the wings, for the wings of a dove.

Her mother and her sister made
The Lillie Trio, and they played
And entertained, with great propriety,
Toronto's most genteel society.

# Beatrice Lillie and Jimmy Durante  Separated at birth?

Bea always dreamed that she'd go far
And be a famous movie star;
She even planned her name as well -
She'd call herself Gladys Montell.

She went to movies all the time
Whenever she possessed a dime.
She little thought one day she'd sing
With Julie Andrews and with Bing.

At boarding school she had no chances
For any nice teenage romances:
Boys came in once a year, to dances.
Bea once led girls in crocodile
Into a bank, to give a smile
To one young teller she preferred -Then
marched them out, without a word.

And then the end of schooldays found
Young Beatrice Lillie London-bound.
The Lillie Trio were together
But disappointment Bea must weather.
She spent her days auditioning
Without achieving anything.
She sang "I hear you calling me" -
Producers, though, did not call Bea.

Then finally she got a call -
A solo spot in Music Hall.

They introduced her to the throng
As Canada's Sweetheart of Song.
The first song that she'd brought along
Was quite a weepie - or a gurgler! -
"Don't steal my prayer-book, Mr Burglar."

She finished, bowed - and to her ears
Came Cockney catcalls, boos and jeers.
Gritting her teeth she carried on
And in the next song, truly shone.
She introduced it with a grin
As "by my friend, Irving Berlin."
And then the audience that jeered her
Eventually stood and cheered her.

Her breakthrough came, the legend goes,
When one of André Charlot's shows
Auditioned singers - Bea was sure
That if she went there looking poor,
A battered suitcase in her hand,
They'd sympathize, and think her grand.

They didn't, till with style and grace
She bowed, and tripped upon the case.
She fell spreadeagled, looking daft -
And those producers, how they laughed!
And she and they perceived it then:
This girl was a comedienne!

And after that she didn't stop:

Quite soon she'd reach the very top.
In musicals and in revues
She made ecstatic headline news;
And then she made more headlines yet
By marrying a Baronet.

Now Beatrice Lillie, she'd reveal,
Was also known as Lady Peel.
Soon after, a Chicago crowd
Bowed back at her, when Beatrice bowed.

Now Beatrice Lillie was the toast
Of audiences coast to coast.
Toronto gave her accolades -
Met her with bands and big parades;
She captivated Europe too
In cabaret and in revue.

Now Charlie Chaplin said her art
Made her his female counterpart,
And Noel Coward wrote specially
Mad Dogs and Englishmen  for Bea.

In Hollywood she found no thrill:
She'd rather be in Vaudeville.
At wartime troop shows she was feted
And by de Gaulle was decorated.

She starred in Thoroughly Modern Millie,
An Evening with Beatrice Lillie,

And then gained even greater fame
By playing the role of Auntie Mame.

Soon audiences for TV
Discovered the delights of Bea.
She had the longest of careers:
It lasted  more than sixty years -
A sign of what her fans did feel
For Beatrice Lillie, Lady Peel.

# JOEY SMALLWOOD
## (1900 – 1991)

*Joey Smallwood rose from poverty to become one of the most flamboyant personalities in Canadian politics, ruling Newfoundland for nearly a quarter of a century. He finally talked his beloved province into joining Canada in 1949, and thus became the last official Father of Confederation.*

Some say it's weird, some say it's grand,
But all agree and understand
There's nowhere quite like Newfoundland.
The BBC in London knew it
And broadcast special programmes to it.

Subject of jokes, and admiration,
It thinks itself a separate nation
With its own music, style of speech
And even its own beverage, *Screech*.
Yes, Newfoundland has always known
It's like a kingdom of its own.

So Joey Smallwood, being no fool,
Decided like a King to rule
For there was nobody more showy
In all of Newfoundland, than Joey.

He said his family for sure
Came from the poorest of the poor –
So, well aware of what he'd missed,

He soon became a socialist.
His oratory, with passion fired,
Had all his audiences inspired.

And Joey's working life, meanwhile,
Was nothing if not versatile:
Newspapers, unions, radio –
At pig farms too he had a go.

And then he saw Canadian unity
As Newfoundland's great opportunity;
So he pursued his high intentions
Through referendums and conventions,
Becoming to his great elation
A Father of Confederation.

As Premier he won election
And people's loyalty and affection,
For his charisma meant they all would
Come out to vote for Joey Smallwood.
Joey his kingly mantle wore
With style, for twenty years and more.

He felt that now he had the chance
His people's fortunes to advance
(With help, of course, from federal grants).
The answer was, in Joey's eyes,
A programme to industrialise.

Although he wasn't one to shirk,
His projects didn't always work.

The fishermen who left the coast
Found town life hadn't much to boast.
Some unions now were shocked to know
That Joey Smallwood was their foe
As he pursued in ruthless fight
The policies he thought were right.

Opponents tried to do him down,
Called him a tyrant and a clown –
And yet his stature just grew bigger
And he became a father figure.
The jaunty style he had perfected
Kept getting Joey re-elected.

In the political arena
Canadians had never seen a
Champion who so boldy jousted –
Until, at last, the Champ was ousted!

Though later on he made a bid
To try to be the Comeback Kid,
He failed, which forced him to admit
An end must come, and this was it.

The politicans might uproot him
But idleness would never suit him,
And Joey didn't find it tedious
To write his huge Encyclopaedias.
Three published volumes of them stand
As lasting tribute, great and grand,
To Joey, King of Newfoundland.

# GUY LOMBARDO
## (1902 – 1977)

*Born in London, Ontario, Guy Lombardo and his brothers*
*formed The Royal Canadians dance band, which became a huge*
*popular success. Their regular New Year's Eve broadcasts became*
*an institution throughout North America and beyond.*

*(If you are in festive mood, these verses can be sung – to the tune,*
*naturally, of Robert Burns's "Auld Lang Syne"...)*

"Should Auld Acquaintance be forgot" –
So sang the festive throng;
And Auld Lang Syne, as many thought,
Was Guy Lombardo's song.

On TV and on radio
It moved them all to tears
When played on Guy Lombardo's show
For nearly fifty years.

Guy's family was musical
And they could all be seen
At gigs in many a local hall
When Guy was just fifteen.

The Royal Canadians was the band
And with it Guy struck gold.
The records boomed in many a land –

One hundred million sold.

Some called his music "syrupy"
But Guy Lombardo swore:
"It is the sweetest there can be
This side of Heaven's door."

For sixty years this sound sublime
Was famed both near and far,
And somehow Guy still found the time
To be a speed-boat star.

So let us hope now Heaven swings
To Guy Lombardo's beat
And angels sweetly pluck the strings
While cherubs tap their feet.

>    For Auld Lang Syne, och aye,
>    For Auld Lang Syne –
>    Let's drink a New Year toast to Guy
>    For Auld Lang Syne!

# JOSEPH-ARMAND BOMBARDIER
## (1908-1964)

*From his teenage years Bombardier showed his creative skill
with machinery, and went on to invent the snowmobile
and the ski-doo, and to found the internationally successful
company that still bears his name.*

All through his childhood and his teens
Bombardier just loved machines.
While other less ingenious boys
Were playing ball or breaking toys
Young Armand's interest was greater
In fiddling with the carburator.
He thought kids' games were just for mugs -
He'd rather clean the sparking plugs.

His father, thinking him a star,
Said, "What a clever lad you are!
So here's an ancient car, my son -
Dismantling it could be fun."

So Armand, grateful to his dad,
Embarked on an idea he had.
He planned a vehicle to go
With passengers, across the snow.

He took the engine out, and fit
Four ski-like runners under it.

Then, being a most inventive feller,
He built himself a large propeller.
With this he would, such was his plan,
Replace the radiator fan.

"Allons, mon petit frère!" he told
His younger brother, Léopold.
Said Armand, "I'll be on the back
To keep the vehicle on track
While at the front end, brother dear,
You sit and use your feet to steer."

Then after each took up his perch
The strange device began to lurch
And judder forward, slowly sliding,
The brothers perilously riding.

Along the snowbound streets they went
Creating great astonishment.
The folk of Valcourt in Quebec
Thought one at least would break his neck.

They zigged and zagged from side to side
While gleefully young Armand cried:
"I had a dream and made it real,
And here it is - the Snowmobile!"

Knowing his genius was large
His father built him a garage
And here with purpose unrelenting

Bombardier went on inventing -
Learned English too, so he could read
The science journals he would need.

The Snowmobile he engineered
Had tracks, and skis in front that steered.
He toured Quebec to flaunt its glories
And featured much in front-page stories.

It met with widespread admiration,
Transforming winter transportation.
Doctors and priests and rescue crews,
The postal service bearing news
And many more, found great appeal
In Armand's wondrous Snowmobile.

Then he devised a new machine:
The Ski-Doo zoomed upon the scene.
A zippy, zappy new sensation,
A must for winter recreation.

His company went on to do
Trains, aeronautics, sea-doos too -
And, honouring Bombardier's fame
The company still bears his name.

Yet no advance in transportation
Could match the wild exhilaration
Of that first journey through the snow
One day in Valcourt, long ago.

The book reads: THE DANGER of SPEAKING DOWN to PEOPLE. JKG

# JOHN KENNETH GALBRAITH
## (born 1908)

*John Kenneth Galbraith was born at Iona Station, Ontario, and educated at Ontario Agricultural College and then at Berkeley and Cambridge University. One of the world's most celebrated economists, he has spent much of his life teaching at Harvard, has been an adviser to several US Presidents, and written many influential books.*

The singular skills of John Kenneth
Have taken him right to the zenith
And there at the peak
With insights unique
What brilliant volumes he penneth!

In stature, John Kenneth Galbraith
Is certainly far from a wraith.
His brain-power and height
Made his rivals look slight –
No wonder his fans have such faith.

His views about things economic
Had an impact no less than atomic
Each treatise and book
Made all other views look
Like something you'd read in a comic!

# MARSHALL McLUHAN
## (1911 – 1980)

*Marshall McLuhan spent most of his academic life at the
University of Toronto, but he gained world-wide renown with his
witty and provocative pronouncements on all aspects of the modern
media and popular culture.*

The schools of Manitoba nourished
The young McLuhan, and he flourished.
At university and college
His brain absorbed prolific knowledge.

He filled his bright, capacious mind
With poetry of every kind,
Much treasure in the Bible found,
And relished Eliot and Pound.

In youth he said: "It's clear to me —
A teacher I shall never be."
But that is just what he became,
A great one, with a world-wide name.

First faced with freshmen, he'd conclude:
"I'm baffled by their attitude.
Their views, morality and such
To me are simply Double Dutch!
To understand their point of view
I must absorb their culture too."

And so began a study which
Would make him famous, praised, and rich.
He beamed his penetrating mind
On media of every kind.

The ads, the soaps, the radio,
The hit parade, the TV show,
Papers and comics, movies, sports,
Were processed in McLuhan's thoughts.

These thoughts his well-known
view would presage —
He said: "The Medium is the Message."
He thought that every new variety
Of medium had changed society.

The advent of the printing press
Had made man's tribal loyalty less.
And now TV, that novel entity,
Would cause us all to lose identity.

Ads were aggressive, he opined:
Sex and technology combined.
And television was pollution —
So really, what was the solution?

We had to understand, he urged,
New media as they emerged.
The rear-view mirror showed, he said,
Only a world that's past and dead.

It's better far to look ahead.

His media studies, as they grew,
Brought him mass audiences too.
This academic was a wow,
A modern media guru now.
Star of the electronic age,
The Global Village was his stage.

To family life and university
He added roles of great diversity.
He flew around on lecture missions,
Advised or hectored politicians,
Wrote copious letters to his friends,
And analysed the latest trends.
He even played, to cap it all,
A walk-on part in Annie Hall!

The media loved him — well, they would:
For sound bites he was always good.
And many companies and firms
Would hire him, on most lavish terms,
To tell them, in his jokey way,
Their practices were all passé.

He said that books, however pleasant,
Were now completely obsolescent.
And some asked why, since he'd so slight them,
He was continuing to write them?

Such barbs he never thought were vexing:
He'd make his answers more perplexing.
He dealt in quips and verbal shocks
And relished puns and paradox.

"Marshall," said one who held him dear,
"Likes churning up the atmosphere;
Provocative and never dumb,
He slugs his critics till they're numb."

And though his fame began to ebb,
The Internet and World Wide Web
May now revive his trenchant theories —
Perhaps they'll make a TV series,
And there McLuhan will survive
And through the Global Village drive
The Information Super Highway,
And cry: "You see — they did it my way!"

# JOE SHUSTER
## (1914-1992)

*Toronto-born Joe Shuster was the artist who created that famous comic-book and screen hero, Superman, still going strong after sixty years.*

When Joe Shuster was a boy
Drawing was his greatest joy.
In Joe's young, fertile mind began
That great creation, SUPERMAN.

With words dreamed up by Jerry Siegal,
The Man of Steel swooped like an eagle
And soon became the scourge of crooks
And hero of the comic books.
He still remained in all his tussles
A man of modesty - and muscles.

It's always said Toronto is
The model for Metropolis;
Toronto's Star  too, if you scan it,
Could have inspired the Daily Planet.
As for Clark Kent, those in the know
Declare that he resembled Joe.

Perhaps Joe, spectacled and shy,
Wished that he too could zoom and fly,

And thought that it would just be bliss
To make that metamorphosis.

What joy to quickly change your shape
And don blue tights and scarlet cape,
An S emblazoned on your chest
So people know that you're the best,
And will defeat the villains now
With many a WHAM! and SPLAT! and POW!
(A phone booth, though, does seem a strange
And rather awkward place to change.)

The hero and his letter S
Became an overnight success.
Was it a bird?  Was it a plane?
And did Clark Kent love Lois Lane?

His hectic role in fighting crime
Left him, of course, so little time -
But they were quite a daunting team,
Frustrating many a deadly scheme:
Those Monsters, Androids, Things from Space -
They quickly put them in their place.

His hero's fame became substantial
But Joe's reward was not financial.
A hundred dollars, that was what
Brave Superman's creator got.
The publishers, to their  delight,
Had bought the total copyright.

Later, when Joe and Jerry Siegal
Maintained the deal had not been legal
And sued to get their hero back
They lost the case, and got the sack.

If only then the x-ray eyes
Of Superman, alert and wise,
Could have observed their misery,
And crying, "Here's a job for me!"
Their hero could have taken flight
And come and seized their copyright!
Sadly, that kind of noble act
Happens in fiction, not in fact.

And now, though his creator's gone
The Man of Steel still carries on.
Although he's over sixty now
He still can WHAM! and ZAP! and POW!
Delighting every ardent fan
Of young Joe Shuster's SUPERMAN.

"The olympics can no more have a deficit than a man can have a baby." Jean Drapeau

# JEAN DRAPEAU
## (1916 – 1999)

*Jean Drapeau was Mayor of Montreal for nearly thirty years,
and dedicated himself to grand and sometimes costly plans
to give the city the style and high profile it still enjoys today.*

Jean Drapeau didn't care to frolic –
In fact, he was a workaholic.
By day and night he gave his all
For his beloved Montreal;
He even slept at City Hall.

Coming to power, he had the aim
To change the city's rakish name,
And many brothels soon were closed
And gambling licences opposed.
Pinball machines were even smashed,
And police corruption too he lashed.

But when the next election came
Opponents blackened Drapeau's name.
In posters now his rivals chose
To show him in a Hitler pose,
And thuggery, intimidation
And dubious vote manipulation
All helped to end Jean Drapeau's reign –
But phoenix-like, he rose again!

This time, to the people's cheers,
He stayed for nearly thirty years.
This most astute of city bosses
Towered like a neat, well-dressed Colossus
And cut a stylish mayoral figure;
Some mayors thought big, but he thought bigger!

A subway, malls deep underground,
Traffic solutions too he found;
Then Expo 67 came
To glorify Jean Drapeau's name.

He even thought there was a chance
To bring the Eiffel Tower from France…
The city did become the home
Of that huge Geodesic Dome,
And fairs and exhibitions all
Brought worldwide fame to Montreal.

But even bigger plans he had –
To host the next Olympiad;
And once the city had been chosen,
Building took off like an explosion –
And as construction grew and grew
The costs began exploding too.

Yet Drapeau's faith remained unsinkable –
A deficit was quite unthinkable.
Although the bills came thick and fast,
Olympic glory came at last.

There in the stadium stood the Mayor,
Now basking in the spotlight's glare.
He raised the flag into the air –
The cheering crowds threw up their chapeaux
To see Mayor Drapeau raise the drapeau!

Later would come recriminations
And budgetary examinations,
But Drapeau with his usual wit,
Said: "This is not a deficit –
I'd rather call it just 'a gap',
And so, why should I take the rap?"

Jean Drapeau for a decade more
With pride his mayoral mantle wore.
Though there were times he gave offence
To some provincial governments
The skilful way he'd wheel and deal
Kept his electoral appeal.

So Drapeau's reign went on and on
Like an Olympic marathon.
No wonder that his fans would call
Jean Drapeau Mister Montreal.

# PIERRE TRUDEAU
## (1919-2000)

*Flamboyant Montreal lawyer Pierre Trudeau became*
*Prime Minister in 1968 and led the country for most of the*
*following sixteen years, during which he was both idolized*
*and reviled, but never ignored.*

Cultured and cool and charismatic,
Pierre's career was never static.
One of the Liberals' leading lights,
He led them up towards the heights;
Then as he basked upon the summit,
His popularity would plummet.
And when it looked like he'd been trounced,
Back to the top he promptly bounced.

Pierre grew up in Montreal;
A schoolboy essay he'd recall:
"What do you want to be?" He thought:
Seaman...? Explorer...? Astronaut...?
(They'd laugh if he had written: "I've
A plan to move to Sussex Drive.")

But Law was what he wound up doing,
And on vacations, went canoeing.
The doctorate plans which he unfurled
Meant travelling around the world —
And so with backpack and with beard

The Hippie Trail he pioneered,
And foiled a knife attacker's bid
While climbing up a Pyramid.
(A useful skill in later life
In worlds where back-stabbing is rife.)

Back home, he saw the great appeal
Of Révolution Tranquille.
The Liberal Party wooed him then
As one of Québec's Three Wise Men.
So, somewhat to his own surprise,
Began his meteoric rise.

Just two years after his election
He stood for leadership selection.
The Old Guard said: "He'll cause us scandals —
The guy wears coloured shirts, and sandals!
Voters will never choose Pierre —
They'd rather have a grizzly bear!"

But they were wrong, that diehard band,
For Trudeaumania swept the land.
It gave the party such a boost,
Soon Pierre Trudeau ruled the roost.
It was the Liberals' finest hour:
The red rose had begun to flower.

The Right looked on with some anxiety
As Trudeau launched his Just Society.
He then said: "Though you may berate us,

We're giving French official status.
The Anglophones must mend their ways
And recognize La Langue Française."

It's no surprise the Opposition
Did not share Trudeau's sense of mission.
He called them "nobodies", a phrase
They hardly took as lavish praise.

One day he mouthed a certain word
In mime, so it could not be heard.
When asked, so there should be no muddle,
What was it? He said: "Fuddle Duddle!
Or really racily, it may be
I might have told you, Fuddle Dee Dee!"

For sixteen years Pierre would reign,
Although his star would wax and wane.
Once, when faintly it did burn,
For nine months, Joe Clark took a turn.

Pierre was showy and dramatic,
Though critics called him autocratic.
"His style," said one, "though he's a stayer,
Makes Judas seem a good team player."

But now and then he got it wrong
With slogans like THE LAND IS STRONG,
To which the voters, like as not,
Were apt to yawn and say: "So what?"

Advisers, in his third campaign,
Said: "Margaret, please don't join the train."
That view she said she would defy;
She called Pierre a loving guy,
And crowds all cheered her to the sky.
But politics would take their toll —
She'd go elsewhere to rock and roll.

Pierre's career went rolling on;
Sometimes he struggled, sometimes shone.
Once, in a ploy both cute and neat,
He engineered his own defeat,
Another time resigned, and then
Decided to come back again.

His progress sometimes could be chequered,
And very nearly got Quebecer'd.
He found it hard to keep in check
The separatists in Quebec,
Tried to maintain a plural nation
And keep them in the Federation —
While other provinces, no doubt,
Were quite inclined to boot them out.

But he survived, to sweat and toil
To solve the crisis over oil,
And eat his words, and eat them whole,
On needs for wage and price control.

But Trudeau, still the clever mover,

The Gang of Eight would outmanoeuvre
And greet with triumph and elation
The Constitution's patriation.

He thought he'd closed that "can of worms",
And later spoke in scathing terms
Of those who opened it to make
Supposed improvements at Meech Lake
And an Accord at Charlottetown.
But then the voters turned them down.

Whether Pierre was loved, or hated,
His style was never understated.
And round the world as he gyrated,
He made quite sure, when he was fêted,
That Canada was highly rated.

Pierre's one of the brighter gems
In lists of Canada's P.M.'s.
Sir John MacDonald was the first —
A great man, with a greater thirst.
He found at last he couldn't handle
The great Pacific Railway scandal.

Then came Mackenzie (Alexander)
A man who was immune to slander.

Translating Gettysburg's Address
Was Wilfrid Laurier, no less —
Abe Lincoln he admired, we knew,

And much admired the ladies too.

The twentieth century would bring
William Lyon Mackenzie King:
The longest serving leader, he
Had one great eccentricity,
For by Ouija board he tried
To reach folks on the Other Side;
His mother, so he claimed, replied.

And then there was rumbustious Dief,
Conservatives' impressive Chief.
Stanfield and Meighen and Joe Clark
To lead the country would embark.
Each made a great or lesser mark.

Lester Pearson did so well,
He got the Peace Prize from Nobel.
From him the leadership would go
Eventually to Pierre Trudeau.

Then Brian Mulroney wheeled and dealed
And quite a fashion sense revealed.
And for a short while, after him,
We caught the briefest glimpse of Kim.

Jean Chrétien took up the fight —
He was a Trudeau acolyte,
So once again the torch could flare
In tribute to the great Pierre!

# JAY SILVERHEELS
## (1919-1980)

*Jay Silverheels grew up on the Six Nations Reserve at Brantford,
Ontario, where he triumphed in many different sports.
He went to Hollywood with a Canadian All-Stars lacrosse team,
and stayed there to become a screen star, especially known for
his role as Tonto in "The Lone Ranger".*

Jay Silverheels, born Harold Smith,
Became a name to conjure with.

A Mohawk whose athletic verve
Made him the star of his Reserve,
He triumphed both on track and field.
Crowds cheered him and opponents reeled
To see the power that he could wield.

His grandfather, a Mohawk chief,
Declared his skills beyond belief
And said, "Henceforth I do decree
Your name Jay Silverheels  shall be."

Young Jay was never at a loss
In hockey, boxing or lacrosse.
At twenty he fulfilled a dream
And toured with a Canadian team,
And their lacrosse was just so good
They were the toast of Hollywood.

There the comedian Joe E. Brown
Persuaded Jay to settle down;
He said, "The claim I want to prove is
That I can get you into movies!"

He did just that, but at the start
Jay only got a walk-on part.
Though he was diligent and dextrous,
`For years he stayed among the extras.

But then at last the breakthrough came:
The role of Tonto made his name.
The masked Lone Ranger could not ride
Without brave Tonto by his side.

His horse was Silver,  and he said
"Hi-yo!" to that great quadruped.
To show he valued human life,
The Ranger, when confronting strife,
Had silver bullets which he used.
The victims must have been confused,
Remarking as they dropped down dead,
"At least the bullet wasn't lead!"

Silver's his theme, the Ranger feels:
For bullets, horse - and Silverheels.

Young audiences thronged to see
The Ranger ride to victory

As he and Tonto did their best
To bring true justice to the West.

In real life Jay helped when he could
Others who came to Hollywood,
And founded, his success to share,
The Indian Actors Workshop there.

Jay and his colleagues' work redressed
The image of the old Wild West
Where noble cowboys were dependable
And savage Indians expendable.

And when he died, they put his name
In Hollywood's big Walk of Fame
Where all the great performers are:
Beside Sinatra's, there's Jay's star -
An all-time tribute that reveals
The talent of Jay Silverheels.

# RENÉ LÉVESQUE
## (1922 – 1987)

*René Lévesque was a celebrated broadcaster before he entered politics as a Liberal. He later founded the Parti Québécois which was victorious in two elections but just failed in 1980 to get a referendum majority in favour of an independent Quebec.*

Though he was small, René Lévesque
Was walking tall throughout Quebec,
Becoming, after many a schism,
The Champion of Separatism.

When he was young, he'd no ambition
To be a party politician.
A war reporter he became –
Then Radio-Canada made his name:
His style and passion brought him fame.

That fame would help him, it was clear,
In a political career;
And so he won a Liberal seat
And joined the Cabinet elite.

At first he backed with resolution
Lesage's Quiet Revolution.
But soon Lévesque would change his tone
And start to strike out on his own,
Fiercely proclaiming to the crowd

A revolution much more loud.

The Parti Québécois was founded
And drums for independence sounded.
Supporters proudly would recall
The words of General de Gaulle:
"Vive le Québec Libre!" was his call
Delivered from the City Hall
When he arrived in Montreal.

It took some years before Lévesque
Was able to persuade Quebec
To opt, in 1976,
For René's brand of politics.

And oh, what rage and consternation
Was felt that day across the nation –
Or anyway, in Ottawa
Where René caused a brouhaha!
He told them, when he heard them yelp:
"A tranquilliser ought to help!"

(Yet there were always those out west
Who thought Quebec was such a pest
It wouldn't really drive them frantic
To see it sink in the Atlantic …)

But René didn't do his worst:
He played it very cool at first,
And talked not of a separate nation,
But "Sovereignty-Association."

This helped his devious intent,
Since no one knew quite what it meant.

René announced, being worldly-wise,
That he'd maintain the federal ties
And promised that he wouldn't end 'em
Until he'd held a Referendum.

He managed to procrastinate
About the question, and the date;
When they were fixed, Quebec would see
Intense campaigns for Non and Oui.

Across the province, to and fro,
They watched the heavy hitters go,
Jean Chrétien and Pierre Trudeau,
Urging the case for voting No.

Although Quebeckers as a whole
Resented federal control,
Sixty per cent of voters stated
They'd no wish to be separated.

Yet when the P.Q. won again
Lévesque's power soon began to wane,
And resignations would conspire
To make him ready to retire.

And now, although Lévesque is gone,
The fights he fought still rumble on.

# MAVIS GALLANT
## (born 1922)

*Mavis Gallant began her writing career with the Montreal*
*Standard, then moved to Paris in 1950 where she continues to*
*write stories, novels and reviews. She had success in France and in*
*the USA but it was some time before she got much recognition at*
*home. Eventually it came, and she won the Governor-General's*
*Award with her collection of Canadian stories, Home Truths.*

The critics agree that on balance
No style can quite match Mavis Gallant's.
She lays pompousness bare
With precision and flair
Which display her satirical talents.

She had a disturbed, restless youth,
And her father she saw as uncouth.
Her Montreal Stories
Show very few glories
But many a bitter Home Truth.

In the paper, she got a big chance
To take up a questioning stance:
"Are Canadians boring?"
"Do plays set them snoring?"
And "Is Marriage killed by Romance?"

She went off to Paris, and wondered

Could she write there, or had she just blun-
dered?
But the stories that came
Made Mavis's name –
The New Yorker took over a hundred.

In her tales of expatriate life
The exiles and misfits were rife.
Each social scene too
Where hypocrisy grew
She probed with an eloquent knife.

At home she was largely ignored
But at last they began to applaud
And now Mavis Gallant
Has found that her talent
Is lauded both here and abroad!

# OSCAR PETERSON
## (Born 1925)

*Born in Montreal, Oscar Peterson was already playing
in bands and on the radio when he was in his teens. With his
flamboyant style and personality, he soon went on to achieve
world-wide popularity and to play with, and be admired by,
all the greatest jazz musicians.*

Oscar, as a virtuoso,
Made other pianists seem just so-so.
This boy who came to wow them all
From London to Carnegie Hall
Was born and raised in Montreal.

Oscar, like all the children, had
Good music lessons from his dad:
He was a porter by profession,
But music was his great obsession.
At school, young Oscar would astound
His fellow-students, gathered round
To hear his boogie-woogie sound.

He won at fourteen, easily,
A contest at the CBC
And soon in his own weekly show
Played piano on the radio.

He wanted to leave school to play;

His father let him have his way,
But said: "Son - be, unlike the rest,
Not just a player, but the Best!"

His father's words young Oscar heeded
And aiming for the top, succeeded.
He played with bands, made records too,
And soon his reputation grew.

Now Oscar got his greatest chance
When he was heard by Norman Granz.
The famous impresario
Declared: "I want you in my show.

Jazz at the Philharmonic's  fame
Will very quickly make your name."
So at Carnegie Hall he played,
And what an impact there he made!
With Ray Brown on the double bass
He quite electrified the place.

From then on, his career was made -
In world-wide concert tours he played.
With Granz's troupe he would appear
In eighty cities in a year.

Crowds reveled at the expertise
Of this magician of the keys.
He seemed to play, his listeners reckoned,
At least a hundred notes a second.

One colleague said: "His pianos seem
So hot, they give off smoke and steam."

This suave and smiling, bear-like man
Was raved about by every fan.
The bracelet that he'd always wear -
A gift to him from Fred Astaire -
Dazzled, just like the watch he wore;
His music dazzled even more.

Practical jokes he played a lot
On colleagues, but revenge they got:
Stuck keys together, even hid
Steel balls inside the piano lid.

Arthritis plagued him, and he'd face
A lot of slurs upon his race.
In Canada he thought it bad
No black was in a TV ad;
Though that today seems very strange,
Oscar's campaign began the change.

At times some music critics panned him -
He said they couldn't understand him.
But though the critics might attack him,
His colleagues never failed to back him.

And Oscar played with all the greats
In Canada and in the States:
With Ella, Armstrong and Count Basie

And Dizzy, always acting crazy.
His various Trios reached the heights
Of challenge and of jazz delights.
Even Art Tatum was impressed
And Art, for Oscar, was the best.

As Oscar now recalls his story,
He ought to bask in all this glory.
A deluge of awards and praise
Honours the way that Oscar plays.

For as one music guru said
When asked: "Who would you like, when dead,
To be reincarnated as?" -
"I would be Oscar, King of Jazz!"

# GORDIE HOWE
## (born 1928)

*Gordie Howe grew up in Saskatchewan, a hockey fanatic
even as a child. His genius was soon spotted by the Detroit Red
Wings, for whom he played for 25 years. His career continued even
after that, and his name appeared constantly in the record books
and is enshrined in Hockey's Hall of Fame.*

The countless fans of Gordie Howe
All thought their hero was a wow.
His hockey prowess showed up soon
Where he grew up in Saskatoon.

There Gordie learned to skate, we're told,
When he was only four years old.
At home, he practised day and night
Shooting with left hand and with right,
And sometimes made his parents grouse
By knocking shingles off the house.

Then by a scout the boy was seen
When he was only just sixteen.
Off to the Red Wings' Camp he'd go
At Windsor in Ontario.

At eighteen, making his debut
His first game saw his first goal too;
The first of many – he would score
In his career, a thousand more.

Bull-necked and burly, Gordie struck
With his fierce stick, not just the puck.
The other players sometimes found
That he had felled them to the ground.

With deadly skill he swooped and scythed
While on the ice his rivals writhed,
And those trapped in the corner knew
The power of Gordie's elbows too.

His whole career was nearly through
When he was only twenty-two:
He skidded, slipped and cracked his head –
Brain damage almost left him dead.
The surgeons saved him – just one trace
Remained – a tic that jerked his face.
His callous team-mates seemed to think he
Would revel in the nickname Blinky!

Soon Gordie's wounds had healed so well
He galvanized the NHL.
Eighty-six points would clearly sock it
To Gordie's runner-up, The Rocket.
His progress after that was stunning
As Scoring Champion four times running.

With Stanley Cups and MVP's
Gordie would lead the field with ease.
This hero, speedy and adroit,
Spent twenty-five years with Detroit.

But his career was not complete:
He managed an amazing feat.

At forty-five, he ruled the roost on
World Hockey's Aero team in Houston,
And – what would really gild the dream –
Gordie's two sons were on the team!

New England and Hartford Whalers too
Brought hockey challenges anew.

No wonder Gordie Howe's great name
Stands out in Hockey's Hall of Fame,
For in that Hall he earned his residence
Through terms of seven U.S. Presidents!

# MAURICE "THE ROCKET" RICHARD
## (1929-2000)

*One of fhe great hockey stars of all time, Maurice Richard played for the Montreal Canadiens for nearly twenty years, broke many records and helped the team to win eight Stanley Cups. He was so popular with the fans that his suspension once caused a riot in the city.*

A Governor-General, called Lord Stanley,
Liked games that were robust and manly.
The fastest, toughest game, he thought,
Was Canada's great winter sport.

Ice hockey first began to thrive
Way back in 1855,
When someone grabbed a hockey stick
And cried: "Now, get your skates on, quick!
Though hockey on the grass is nice,
We'll play it faster on the ice."

It caught on quickly, and became
A favourite Canadian game.
Lord Stanley never ever tired
Of seeing the game he so admired.
He said: "I'd love to take it up,
But I'm an old dog, not a pup:
Instead, I shall present a Cup."

And so the Stanley Cup was made,
And for it fierce, fast games are played:
Tumultuous, titanic clashes
Where every player swerves and dashes
And swoops and darts and sometimes crashes.
Defeat and danger they defy,
Hoping to hold that trophy high.

Now, Hockey's crowded Hall of Fame
Resounds with many a famous name.
Among the greatest, many claim,
To reach the summit of the game
Rocket Richard's best of all —
Canadiens' star, in Montreal.

It was in 1942
The Rocket first soared into view,
And fans of the Canadiens
Watching him play, exclaimed: "Tiens!
Maurice va jouer très bien!"

And they were right — for eighteen years
The Forum rang with rapturous cheers
As, blazing forth in every game,
The Rocket really earned his name.

Just two years after he'd begun
The team sure made those Red Wings run:
The record score was 9 to 1.
A game to come was better still —

A play-off, won Eleven-Nil.

The Final of the Stanley Cup
In '52 lined two teams up:
Boston and Montreal were playing;
Canadiens' fans were surely praying —
They couldn't bear it if they lost on
Such a night, to rivals Boston.

Each team was full of brave defiance —
This was a battle of the giants.
The scores were even for a spell;
A heavy tackle — Maurice fell!
Knocked out and bloody, he revived —
The tie-break finally arrived.

The winning goal the Rocket scored:
Fans cheered the hero they adored.
The crowd stood up, and that ovation
Was four whole minutes in duration.

Many times since, those rival Bruins
Were left with their defence in ruins;
And there were lots of other teams
Who left the ice with shattered dreams.
Canadiens' goals inspired the Forum,
And Maurice knew just how to score 'em.

Richard his name has also lent
To one unfortunate event,

The Richard Riot, which we know
Was more than forty years ago.

A fight had happened on the ice —
Richard's behaviour wasn't nice.
Said Hockey's President: "Richard —
From all this season's games, you're barred!"

The President's decision came
The night before a Red Wings game.
The fans thought this appalling manners,
And marched the streets with protest banners.
President Campbell rashly came
To take his seat to watch the game.

The fans, who thought he was the dregs,
Threw ripe tomatoes, rocks and eggs.
By someone's fist he soon got hit,
And then a tear gas bomb was lit.
The place filled up with yellow smoke;
The crowd began to scream and choke.

The game was lost, the fans went out
And roared and raged and rushed about.
Windows were smashed, cars overturned,
Shops looted, and some buildings burned.
The rioting went on all night,
And left the city quite a sight.

Though Maurice wanted no such show

And asked for calm, on radio,
The Richard Riot always came
To be remembered with his name.

The next year, that same President
The Stanley Cup would soon present
To Maurice, for his winning team:
A nightmare turned into a dream.
And then, from there the team would go
To win four more Cups in a row.

More records saw him top the polls:
The first to get five hundred goals,
And first to score, of all great names,
His fifty goals in fifty games.
Eight Stanley Cups he helped to win;
First TV coverage he was in.

His reputation — none would knock it,
For there's been no one like The Rocket!

# GLENN GOULD
## (1932 – 1982)

*Toronto-born Glenn Gould could play the piano when he was three,
compose at five, and went to the Royal Conservatory of Music
when he was ten. Making his debut at thirteen, he was soon a star
of the concert stage, which he eventually gave up to devote all his
time to recording. His playing style was as individual as his
lifestyle, and his recordings particularly of Bach's keyboard works
are admired throughout the world.*

For months, while Glenn was in the womb,
His mother in the living-room
Would play the piano every day;
She thought this was the neatest way
To give the child a perfect start
In mastering the pianist's art.

It seems that she was right, for he
Was playing by the age of three.
This infant prodigy, before
He read words, learned to read a score.
Toronto's Royal Conservatory
Gave Glenn, at fourteen, a degree.

And soon Glenn Gould was all the rage,
A star on every concert stage.
The audiences he'd amaze,
Not least with his eccentric ways.

In rumpled clothes he'd sway about
His long wild hair all sticking out.
Conducting gestures too he made
And hummed the music as he played.

And when Glenn Gould began recording
The fans' response was most rewarding.
He'd sleep by day, record at night,
And edit tapes till they were right.
Each phrase was shaped, no note was missed –
Glenn Gould was a perfectionist.

Then suddenly at thirty-one
He shocked and startled everyone:
"I'll play no more on stage!" he said,
"The concert hall will soon be dead!"
Glenn would no longer be on show –
Out of the limelight he would go,
A hermit in his studio.

He did emerge, his tales to tell
In films, and radio shows as well,
Which were as quirky and bizarre
As Glenn's style as a piano star.

His clothes were quite eccentric too:
He'd dress for winter, all year through.
Milkshakes and custard were his diet;
At night his phone was never quiet:
His friends would listen with great patience

To hours of late-night conversations.

The eighty albums Glenn Gould made
Continue to be loved and played.
And yet one day he told a friend:
"I think my funeral at the end
Will not of course attract a throng."
Let's hope he knows now he was wrong:
His fans in hundreds came along.

And Glenn Gould's music found a place
In capsules sent to Outer Space.
So maybe, in a million years
Some alien, exotic ears
Will, on a planet far away
Hear Glenn performing Bach, and say:
"Those Earthlings sure knew how to play!"

# NORVAL MORRISSEAU
## (born 1932)

*Norval Morrisseau grew up on the Sand Point Reserve
in Ontario. A self-taught artist, he painted the legends of his
Ojibwa heritage on birch-bark and paper. They were seen by
an art dealer who brought them to his gallery in Toronto
for an exhibition which made Morrisseau an instant success,
as well as a huge influence in the Canadian art world.*

First Nations were indeed the first
In art and culture to be versed
And long before the whites arrived
Their painting and their carving thrived.

The new arrivals sent those Nations
To go and live on reservations
And there, though poor and most deprived,
Their art and culture still survived.

The Europeans lived apart
And had their own ideas of Art
And so they never got acquainted
With what the native artists painted.

But then Jack Pollock got to know
The work of Norval Morrisseau
In far north-west Ontario.
On birch-bark and on paper too

In strong, bright images he drew
Ojibwa legends which he knew:

Tales of creation, death and birth,
And human struggles here on Earth –
world where spirits can reside
With human beings, side by side.

One thing made his work stand apart,
As Pollock saw, from other art
Which durably and firmly stood
Painted or carved in stone or wood:
These works of Norval Morrisseau
Could be removed and put on show.

And so in 1962
Toronto's art world got to view
A vision startling and new
That came from the Ojibwa Nation
And caused at once a big sensation.

Now overnight the painter came
From poverty to wealth and fame
And Morrisseau was quite surprised
To find himself so lionized.

He'd given Art a fresh dimension
That broke with custom and convention.
Now other Nations' artists too
Adapted Norval's style and view

And Morrisseau had been the start
Of one whole school called Woodland Art –
And now their culture could expect
New understanding and respect.

But Norval Morrisseau would find
Not everyone would be so kind:
At home he'd hear some elders say
Their myths should not be on display.

But Morrisseau went on meanwhile
To shape his individual style
And Expo 67 came
To give his work a world-wide fame.

He'd played his pioneering part
And caused at last the world of Art
To view with new appreciation
The culture of his ancient Nation.

# THE DIONNE QUINTS
## (born 1934)

*The Dionne Quints were the first identical quintuplets to survive.*
*Their birth in a farmhouse at Callander, Ontario, caused a*
*worldwide sensation, and brought the family fame and fortune,*
*and many problems too.*

The thought of giving birth to Quints
Would make a lot of mothers wince.
When Madame Dionne had her five
No-one believed they could survive.

For they were in a desperate plight:
No water or electric light
Was in the farmhouse where all night
Their mother laboured, giving birth
To this new wonder of the earth.

The doctor and the midwives strove
To warm the Quints before a stove.
A basket there was all they got
To make a cramped and crowded cot.
Their father felt a bit unsteady:
He'd seven children there already.

After a week, the weight they'd reach
Was little more than two pounds each.

And yet Annette and Emilie
Yvonne and Cécile and Marie
Survived to be a famous show
In Callander, Ontario,
And guaranteed the world would know
Of Doctor Allan Roy Dafoe.

For soon a gaggle of reporters
Was swarming round the Dionne daughters.
The newsreels whirred, the flashbulbs popped,
The hectic circus never stopped.
The doctor greeted with felicity
The massive media publicity.

Chicago's World Fair then reacted -
And soon they had Dionne contracted.
Off to the Fair the Quints would go,
Five little stars to steal the show.
But then the Government said "No!"

Ontario's rulers, quick to see
A golden opportunity,
Said, "For the Quints' sake, we declare
We're going to take them into care."

The Quints from home were quickly moved:
The public and the press approved.
They thought it only right - and so
Did Doctor Allan Roy Dafoe.

A hospital was soon erected
Just so the Quints could be protected.
They needed, in the doctor's view,
Protection from their parents too.
In theory they could come to call,
But were not welcomed there at all.
They tried to move in, feeling sore -
But very soon were shown the door.

And yet Dafoe, the Quints' physician,
Said they could go on exhibition.
Inside the hospital was made
A place where they could be displayed.
The children played there in their crèche;
Around the sides, a fine wire mesh
Screened off the eager public, who
Filed slowly past them, peering through.

To see the children, thousands came
To Quintland, as it soon became.
Their dresses must be all the same,
Which led psychologists to claim
Each had no individual role
But looked like guppies in a bowl.

Their guardians ignored such strictures
And put them into motion pictures;
And clearly they were perfect for
Endorsing products by the score.

Milk by Carnation, Oats by Quaker,
Even a disinfectant-maker,
Toothpaste and mattresses and soap
All found a new commercial scope
And soaring sales, upon the basis
Of those five small, cherubic faces.

The locals basked in all this glory:
In books the midwives sold their story.
In Mr Dionne's shop you'd find
Cheap souvenirs of every kind.
He also had a woolen shop,
While the garage where cars would stop
Had five  pumps - yes, you get the hint -
Each named after a Dionne Quint.

Their father waged a big campaign
To get the children back again.
It took nine years though, to convince
The world that he should have the Quints.

At last opinion swung his way:
Public and press could now portray
The place made for the Quints to dwell
As very like a prison cell.

The guardians said that there should be
A new house for the family.
The parents then were quite delighted:
They and the Quints were reunited.

But there was little happiness:
Their freedom now was even less.
Their father never let them roam
Outside the fence around their home,
 And even kept two bears that growled
At any onlooker who prowled.
Their father, stern and quick to blame,
Still made the Quints all dress the same.

At eighteen they were sent away
To convent school at Nicolet.
Emilie died - her sisters, all
Grief-stricken, moved to Montreal;
And though their parents took it hard
The daughters sent no Christmas card.

Now trust fund arguments were rife
And legal battles dogged their life.
They said then, looking from a distance:
"Money, not love, ruled our existence."

Although such births are now not rare,
There've been no siblings anywhere
So famous, or unlucky, since
Ontario's five Dionne Quints.

# LEONARD COHEN
## (born 1934)

*Leonard Cohen grew up in an affluent family in Montreal,
went to university at McGill and Columbia, and was
one of the group of radical writers who transformed the
Canadian poetry scene. He became a singer and songwriter and
since his first record appeared in 1968 has kept a large and loyal
following of enthusiastic fans in many countries.*

Leonard Cohen wrote some poetry
   when he was just a student
And his words they were not tame
   and his words they were not prudent
His classy Westmount background
   he would never let deter him
As an avant-garde protester
   he knew fans would much prefer him.

Soon Leonard started singing
   and he gathered quite a following
In his pool of melancholia
   they were happy to be wallowing
His sombre way of dressing
   couldn't make him look much starker
And his glasses they were dark
   and yet his songs were even darker

And they loved to travel with him

for they knew that they would find
He had saddened everybody
  with his mind.

His lyrics could be baffling
  but he never wrote a platitude
Even when he sampled substances
  designed to change your attitude
He was seeking sacred pathways
  and he wondered where they ended
But no faith appealed to Leonard
  even half as much as Zen did.

His forlorn farewells to lovers
  had a hundred variations
Suzanne and Marianne
  just had to hear them out with patience
Though the tunes were somewhat similar
  and the lovers could be scornful
What made the fans delighted
  was that all of them were mournful

And they loved to travel with him
  for they knew that they would find
He had saddened everybody
  with his mind.

# DONALD SUTHERLAND
## (born 1935)

*Donald Sutherland grew up in Bridgewater, Nova Scotia,*
*and went to the University of Toronto as an engineering student*
*before his acting talents led him to take up theatre. He moved from*
*stage to film, and a long and versatile career in over a hundred*
*movies which have made him an international star.*

Oh what a credit to his Motherland
Is movie actor Donald Sutherland!
His acting talent was precocious,
This famous son of Nova Scotia's.

Though earlier in his career
He studied as an engineer,
He found the theatre's allure
More dazzling, if much less secure.

He went to England, where he trained
And early stage experience gained;
And then he turned to film instead:
The Castle of the Living Dead
Was Gothic stuff, in horrors rich –
And in it, Donald played a witch.

After more horror movie thrills
He showed his comic acting skills:
The Dirty Dozen was a smash,

Then came his biggest breakthrough, MASH.
As Hawkeye, Sutherland became
A celebrated movie name.

He's acted since without a break:
Five films a year he'd sometimes make.
More than a hundred movies now
Have seen our Donald take a bow

And demonstrated his ability
And quite amazing versatility.

Robbers, detectives, firebugs, spies –
His roles were often a surprise.
The painter Gauguin he portrayed
And Jesus Christ he also played.

He says he is a great respecter
Of all the skills of the director.
"A movie actor's there," he's stated,
"To like to be manipulated."
To back his reverential claims
He gave his kids directors' names.

Donald in recent times has been
Back home upon the theatre scene.
When asked: "Does theatre cause you stress?"
He answered very firmly: "Yes!
Film acting's stressful in its way –
Sometimes you throw up every day!
On stage you're stressed when you appear –
It's just a different kind of fear.
But both have got as compensation
Their own immense exhilaration."

So Donald Sutherland continues
To flex his strong artistic sinews,
Enhancing with his gleaming radiance
The galaxy of star Canadians!

# Tonite!
# JONI
# MITCHELL

**Sorry! Parking lot is full**

Glenvale
# Auditorium

# JONI MITCHELL
## (born 1943)

*Joni Mitchell grew up in Saskatoon where she first performed
in coffee houses. Later in Toronto and then in Los Angeles
her individual style and original songs made her a star on
the performance circuit and on records.*

Joni was born in Fort MacLeod
And made her parents very proud.
She later said they'd counted on
A boy they'd christen Robert John,
But when the baby's sex was known
They changed it to Roberta Joan.

Some frugal times the family knew
In prairie towns where Joni grew.
She suffered a near-fatal blow
At nine years old, from polio;
But struggling bravely, she survived
And as a lithe teenager thrived.

She loved the party dancing scene,
Won contests as a Teenage Queen
And listened to rock music daily -
Then bought herself a ukulele.

Though modern styles did not come soon
To prairie towns like Saskatoon

Its coffee house, Louis Riel,
Was where the trendier types did well.

There Joni started her career;
Most liked her, although some would sneer.
At least she earned enough reward
To mean that now she could afford
 A real guitar, which all were thinking
Outclassed the ukulele's plinking.

And with this brand-new instrument
She started to experiment.
Eccentric tuning styles she made
To match whatever song she played,
And found her voice could quickly change
To span a most impressive range.

That range made Joni quite unique:
Like birds that glide from peak to peak
Ruling their kingdom in the sky
Her voice swooped low or soared up high.

"She sounds," one critic chose to grouse,
"Like someone swallowing a mouse!"
But many others found her voice
As classy as the best Rolls Royce.

Her toothy smile, her long blonde hair,
Made her distinctive everywhere.
In 1967 came

Her Chart success, The Circle Game.
Then with her reputation growing
She found she had the Urge for Going.

From town to town she made her way:
Toronto, New York, then L.A.
In Laurel Canyon there she stayed
And wrote the moving songs she played
And found she had a fortune made:
For writing songs and then recording
Had proved for Joni most rewarding.

She formed a lucrative creation,
Her own big music corporation;
And just to make the fortune swell
She purchased real estate as well.
She said, "I'm now, by some strange twist,
The only hippie capitalist!"
Relationships were less secure,
And restless Joni used to tour -
Guitar-case crammed with routes and maps
And lyrics scrawled on paper scraps.

Star rock groups Joni moved among
Like Crosby, Stills and Nash and Young -
Found love and lost it, went abroad
Where thousands gathered to applaud,
Spent time in Crete where hippie raves
Were held among the mountain caves.

But not all Joni's ways were wild -
Her life was often calm and mild:
She liked to cook and paint and knit,
Play cribbage when she'd time for it.

While as for fame, it waxed and waned.
Sometimes as Queen of Rock she reigned,
Her records reaching such success
Elvis himself was selling less.
Though sometimes too we must confess
She languished in the wilderness.

Now, Joni Mitchell's here to stay -
Grammy Awards have come her way
And most of all, her fans in throngs
Remember Joni's subtle songs:

Her poetry of love that ends,
Of hope and freedom, fickle friends,
Dreams of a river to skate away on,
Of Chelsea Mornings to greet the day on,
Of the paradise we haven't got,
Now paved to make a parking lot.
As one enamoured critic found:
"If angels sang, that's how they'd sound!"

# GILLES VILLENEUVE
## (1950-1982)

*Born in Quebec, Gilles Villeneuve was a champion snowmobile*
*racer before he took up motor-racing. His daredevil style on*
*the Formula Atlantic and Formula One circuits, as well as*
*his personal charm, made him a hugely popular figure in Canada*
*and abroad. He was killed in a collision at the age of 32,*
*but his name lives on in Montreal's Grand Prix Circuit and*
*in the motor-racing triumphs of his son Jacques.*

No racer was faster than Gilles
He had such magnetic appeal
    He first took the lead
    At phenomenal speed
When he raced in his sleek snowmobile
    VROOM, VROOM!

When he went into Formula Atlantic
His prowess was truly gigantic
    In one year, he'd first places
    In nine major races
And the fans' jubilation was frantic!
    VROOM, VROOM!

In flying, snowmobiling or driving
He was mostly the first one arriving
    The risks that he'd take
    Would make other men quake

For on danger he felt he was thriving!
VROOM, VROOM!

And when to Ferrari he'd gone
His star in Grand Prix races shone
His career was cut short
In this perilous sport
But Villeneuve's name will live on -
VROOM, VROOM!

# BRET "HITMAN" HART
## (born 1957)

*Bret Hart grew up in Calgary in a family of wrestlers:*
*his father Stu ran the celebrated Stampede Circuit for many years.*
*He has won the World Heavyweight Championship title six times,*
*and was a key figure in the battles for control between*
*the two big wrestling federations, as well as appearing in*
*film documentaries and TV drama series.*

The champion, Bret "Hitman" Hart,
Always looked like a star from the start.
With his hold, the Sharpshooter,
His rivals he'd neuter
And tear them all slowly apart.

Bret's father the wrestler would say:
"Our cellar's ideal for the fray."
He had his boys plungin'
Down into 'The Dungeon'
To practise for five hours a day.

When Bret as a pro was appearing
His boyish good looks were endearing;
Though his hair in the headlocks
Was like stringy dreadlocks
His charm had the fans up and cheering.

His athletic and muscular bulk

Could cause other wrestlers to sulk.
In his dashing pink tights
He won legions of fights
With guys like King Kong, Snake, and Hulk.

Every wrestler must have the appeal
Of a good "Babyface" or bad "Heel".
Though their falls, like a dance,
Are all planned in advance,
The blood that they shed is for real!

Bret's wrestling career was to bring
Many fights, in and out of the ring –
But his fame it still grows
And all Calgary knows
That their local boy is the King!

# WAYNE GRETZKY
## (born 1961)

*When still in his teens, Wayne Gretzky began his spectacular career with the Edmonton Oilers, helping them to win four Stanley Cups in five years. He later joined the Los Angeles Kings and the St Louis Blues. He broke over sixty NHL records and went on to be honoured as the best hockey player of all time – "The Great One".*

A jersey labelled 99
Was lifted up on high
To shouts and cheers and many tears
When Gretzky said goodbye.

The man they call The Great One –
A name he truly earned –
Always so proud to please the crowd,
To Edmonton returned.

For here his greatest triumphs
Those cheering crowds inspired.
It was a blow for them to know
That Gretzky had retired.

This skinny kid from Brantford
Fulfilled his boyhood dream
And made his name and gained his fame
Upon the Oilers' team.

The hockey records tumbled
The scores they mounted up.
The sparkling goals arrived in shoals
So did the Stanley Cup.

He scored more goals than anyone
In all the NHL.
He never missed with his assists –
Oh how those records fell!

The day that Wayne and Janet
Up to the altar went,
The grand parades and accolades
Were like a royal event.

Wayne Gretzky's sporting image
Was always squeaky clean,
So he got lots of TV spots
For products on the screen.

He also played for Canada
With passion and with pride:
The Maple Leaf in his belief
Adorned the greatest side.

And in the States, the President
Would even bow before him:
He was so famed that Reagan claimed
He'd swap all Texas for him!

"Just one more year!" the fans all cried,
"You're greatest of the Greats!"
Wayne said: "The Hall of Fame has all
My hockey sticks and skates!"

"So farewell to you, hockey fans,
For I must leave you now."
The rafters shook as Gretzky took
His last and final bow.

# PAMELA ANDERSON
## (born 1967)

*Born in Ladysmith, British Columbia, Pamela Anderson became
celebrated as a buxom adornment of magazines and then as a star
of the television series "Baywatch". Her career and her personal life
seem to have been conducted in a constant spotlight of publicity.*

In Playboy Pam was all the rage
As she came busting from the page;
In Baywatch no one could ignore her –
Once more she carried all before her.

Beaches seem central to her life,
For on one, she became a wife.
Clad only in a swimsuit, she
Married the rocker, Tommy Lee.

The pair did not exactly try
To stay out of the public eye:
After one amorous airplane trip
They claimed Mile-High Club membership,
And steamy scenes would somehow get
Exposed upon the Internet.

Pam had breast implants in, then out –
Events the papers wrote about,
Just as they told the sordid tale

Of Tommy ending up in jail
For beating Pamela – in due course
The marriage ended in divorce.

But later, saying that he went
To train in Anger Management
Tommy regretted his attack
And wanted Pam to take him back.
Where could this touching plea be seen –
Where else but on the TV screen?

It seems that Pamela was viewing:
Instead of crying: "Nothing doing!"
She liked this very public wooing
And planned to wed again, once more
On a Pacific Ocean shore.

They chose a beach in Malibu
To say again the words "I do."
This time they'd really have a ball
And wed with nothing on at all.

Could this be naked eccentricity
Or one more chance to get publicity?
It is a far cry, certainly,
From life in Ladysmith, B.C.

# CELINE DION
## (born 1968)

*Celine Dion grew up in Charlemagne, Quebec,*
*in a musical family, and composed her first song at the age*
*of twelve. She went on to become a world-famous singing star,*
*selling millions of records and winning Oscars for movie theme*
*songs, as well as a host of other awards.*

"My heart," declared Celine Dion,
"Will certainly go on and on,
And on and on and on and on,
Just like the endless song I sang
The night the ship's alarm bells rang
And everyone began to panic
Aboard the stately, doomed Titanic.
My voice of course remained to float
Upon the waves – unlike the boat."

This future star pop-music queen
Was born the youngest of fourteen.
At five, the tuneful tot would be
Performing with the family –
An infant prodigy was she.

When she was twelve, Celine Dion
Composed her very first chanson.
For René Angelil, the demo
Caused him to say: "Now, take a memo!

This little girl is going far –
I plan on making her a star.
And to be sure her records sell,
I'll be her manager as well."

So in her teens the young Celine
Was launched upon the music scene.
She very quickly reached the top
And then she never seemed to stop.

Most of the songs Celine recorded
With praise and prizes were rewarded.
Some envious glances she might get
From Shania Twain and Morrissette
But as for rivals, she could flatten 'em
With countless discs of gold and platinum.

Albums like Falling into You
Meant her success just grew and grew.
An Oscar came when she released
The theme for Beauty and the Beast.

Let's Talk About Love was one big title –
And to her, love was always vital.
It featured in most everything
Celine composed or chose to sing.

Some critics, looking for her faults,
Said she was wallowing in schmaltz;
One even dared compare her sound

To being in maple syrup drowned.

Love ruled her music, and her life,
For she became her guru's wife:
René she wed, once and for all,
At Notre Dame, in Montreal.

Not once and for all, as things turned out:
In case there should be any doubt,
Just five years later they'd decide
To act again as groom and bride.
A farewell concert she would do
(The latest one of quite a few)
Then to Las Vegas they were heading
To stage a most flamboyant wedding.

A ballroom was, for this event,
Transformed into a Bedouin tent.
Celine's dress looked like gold enamel
And dazzled every watching camel.

Jugglers performed, musicians played,
A belly-dancer writhed and swayed.
The pair on chairs were carried in
And then the wedding could begin.
They both held candles, then drank up
In turn, wine from a golden cup.

The ritual wasn't over yet:
They each put on a coronet,

And all this weird, elaborate show
Took up twelve pages in "Hello!"

Now some, bored by the goings-on
Of René and Celine Dion
Might only hope, with many a sigh,
This time, "Hello!" might mean: "Goodbye!"
Though others think that outlook's noir
And would prefer an "Au Revoir!"

# SASQUATCH

*The Sasquatch, also known as Bigfoot, is a tall hairy creature believed to inhabit the mountains and forests of the Canadian and American northwest. Many sightings have been reported and many footprints found, but scientists are still not certain whether the Sasquatch and its similar Himalayan counterpart, the Yeti, are mythical or real.*

The Sasquatch, so the story goes,
Has long arms, and a wide, flat nose.
He walks tall — there's no doubt of that —
He's nine feet high, without a hat.

Though tales of his appearance vary,
They all agree he's very hairy.
His four-foot chest is like a wall,
He seems to have no neck at all:
In fact, his build would make him seem
A natural for the football team.

His big toe's huge, his feet the same;
No wonder, when he rose to fame,
That BIGFOOT was his other name.

In folklore, though it's hardly science,
He is descended from the Giants
Who fought in two ferocious bands
Among the northwest forest lands.

Their gentler offspring, legends say,
Roam in those mountain woods today.

Some claim he's cousin to the Yeti
Whose footprints, scattered like confetti,
Make disbelief seem simply petty.
But skeptics still maintain that no men
Have seen Abominable Snowmen.

The Bigfoot Sasquatch, though, has been
By many different people seen.
Even a film for one whole minute
Has claimed to have the creature in it.
This claim some scientists refute
And say the figure, though hirsute,
Is someone in a monkey suit.

Earlier, miners in a shack
Claimed they'd been subject to attack.
When skeptics said, once more aloof:
"If that's a Sasquatch, where's the proof?"
The miners growled: "Then who, you goof,
Spent all night pounding on the roof?"

One Albert Ostman claimed that he
At Toba Inlet, in B.C.,
Was kidnapped by a family.
One night when he was camping out
A giant Sasquatch lurked about,
And gathered up his gear, then crept

And picked up Ostman as he slept.

He took him home to meet the wife,
And Ostman shared their Sasquatch life.
Their son and daughter too were there:
The captive was a sight so rare
They never ceased to laugh and stare.

Although they offered him no harm,
He found the life had little charm.
He slipped away into the distance —
At least he'd proof of their existence!
The only proof, though, was his word,
And few believed in what they heard.

In spite of countless sightings more
And sets of prints of feet galore
The skeptics say that these alone
Are not enough, just on their own.
They say that not one hair or bone
Or even tooth has once been shown.

So where have all the Sasquatch gone?
The controversy rages on.
Are Yetis, Bigfoots, and Sasquatches
Seen only after several scotches?

Are they as fictional as Chaucer,
Or creatures from a Flying Saucer?
And more believable or less

Than Monsters living in Loch Ness?

Perhaps they're prudently deciding
It's safer if they stay in hiding.
Who wants to be coralled in zoos,
Or pictured on the TV News?

Perhaps the truth we'll never know.
There's one big question lurking, though:
However we may fret and fuss,
Do Sasquatches believe in us?

# OMNIBUS

Author's note

Aislin and I have so much enjoyed our collaboration on our three books of verses about Canadians past and present, it is a great delight to us that our publisher Kim McArthur has decided to bring them all together in this combined edition.

What an impressive gallery of characters they are! And what a tribute to the enormous vitality, courage and eccentricity of the people who helped to shape this very individual nation. We hope you will enjoy this extraordinary assembly of artists, writers, adventurers, inventors, pirates, tycoons, politicians, sporting stars and sheer mavericks.

My thanks for their assistance in my research go to the Canadian Embassy in Dublin and the London Library, as well as to Marsha Boulton for her entertaining series of *Just A Minute* biographies, and to friends like Michael Phillips and William Agar for their help and advice.

Most of all I want to thank Aislin for his wonderfully funny and shrewd illustrations, Mary Hughson for her excellent work on the book's design, and Kim McArthur for all her buoyant enthusiasm, encouragement and constant inspiration.

*Gordon Snell*